JAMES HILLMAN UNIFORM EDITION

1

JAMES HILLMAN

ARCHETYPAL PSYCHOLOGY

SPRING PUBLICATIONS
PUTNAM, CONN.

Uniform Edition of the Writings of James Hillman
Volume 1

Published by Spring Publications, Inc.
www.springpublications.com

Originally published in Italian in 1981 as "Psicologia archetipica," a chapter in Volume V of the *Enciclopedia del Novecento*. First published in English language as *Archetypal Psychology: A Brief Account* in 1983.

Revised and expanded fourth edition, 2013

Cover illustration:
James Lee Byars, *Untitled,* ca. 1960. Black ink on Japanese paper.
Estate of James Lee Byars, courtesy Michael Werner Gallery, New York, London, Berlin.

Library of Congress Cataloging-in-Publication Data

Hillman, James.
Archetypal psychology / James Hillman. – Revised and expanded fourth edition.
    pages cm. – (Uniform edition of the writings of James Hillman ; 1)
Includes bibliographical references.
ISBN 978-0-88214-998-1 (clothbound : alk. paper)
1. Archetype (Psychology) 2. Psychoanalysis. I. Title. II. Series: Hillman, James. Works. 2013 ; 1.
BF175.H458 2013
150.19'54–dc23
                            2013034458

∞ The paper used in this publication meets the minimum requirements of the American National Standard for Information Sciences – Permanence of Paper for Printed Library Materials, ANSI Z39.48-1992.

The Uniform Edition of the Writings of James Hillman
is published in conjunction with

Dallas Institute Publications, Joanne H. Stroud, Director

The Dallas Institute of Humanities and Culture
Dallas, Texas

an integral part of its publications program concerned with
the imaginative, mythic, and symbolic sources of culture.

Additional support for this publication has been provided by

The Fertel Foundation, New Orleans, Louisiana

Pacifica Graduate Institute, and
Joseph Campbell Archives and Library,
Carpinteria, California

Contents

Prefatory Note

James Hillman prefaced the first English edition of *Archetypal Psychology: A Brief Account*, published in 1983, with the following note:

> This monograph was written during the autumn of 1979 at the request of the Istituto dell'Enciclopedia Italiana for inclusion in Volume V of the *Enciclopedia del Novecento*, published in 1981, where it can be read in the Italian translation of Bianca Garufi. Her assiduous attention helped these condensed formulations find their final expression. Though I feel ambivalent about these sorts of abbreviations, it seemed to me that since it was out in translation, why not in the original. For this first publication in English, I have made scarcely any revisions, neither bringing the literature up to date (other than a few insertions), nor enumerating the directions archetypal psychology has taken in various hands since 1979, nor reporting on lectures, conferences, meetings. Developments move so quickly that the fantasy of "keeping up to date" is misplaced.
>
> Rather, this essay serves merely to locate archetypal psychology as a topic of thought presented in the style of an encyclopedia of the twentieth century.

Since its first publication, *Archetypal Psychology: A Brief Account* has been republished several times. For the 1997 edition, the bibliography of sources and works in the field of archetypal psychology, patiently compiled by Thomas Cheetham, was significantly expanded. The list of Hillman's published writings was revised and cross-referenced with meticulous attention by Joan Luster. Further revisions to the list were made in 2004, when *Archetypal Psychology* became the first volume of the Uniform Edition of the Writings of James Hillman.

Shortly after the publication of the 2004 edition, the complete list of Hillman's writings contained in *Archetypal Psychology* was published online as part of the James Hillman Collection in the Opus Archives and Research Center, where it is freely accessible at *www.opusarchives.org/hillman_bibliography.shtml*.

In early 2011, Hillman requested that in the next edition the list of his writings be removed (since it is now maintained online at Opus), and three additional texts be included instead, which he felt belonged in this introductory account of archetypal psychology: "Why 'Archetypal Psychology'?"; "Psychology: Monotheistic or Polytheistic?"; and "Psychology: Monotheistic or Polytheistic? – Twenty-Five Years Later."

Wherever possible, bibliographical references have been updated to the most recent editions and translations, and some relevant works published after 2004 have also been added.

– Klaus Ottmann

Part One

A Brief Account

1

Sources of Archetypal Psychology

Archetypal psychology, first named as such by James Hillman (1970*b*), had from its beginning the intention of moving beyond clinical inquiry within the consulting room of psychotherapy by situating itself within the culture of Western imagination. It is a psychology deliberately affiliated with the arts, culture, and the history of ideas, arising as they do from the imagination. The term "archetypal," in contrast to "analytical," which is the usual appellation for Jung's psychology, was preferred not only because it reflected "the deepened theory of Jung's later work that attempts to solve psychological problems beyond scientific models" (Hillman 1970*b*); it was preferred more importantly because "archetypal" belongs to all culture, all forms of human activity, and not only to professional practitioners of modern therapeutics. By traditional definition, archetypes are the primary forms that govern the psyche. But they cannot be contained only by the psyche, since they manifest as well in physical, social, linguistic, aesthetic, and spiritual modes. Thus, archetypal psychology's first links are with culture and imagination rather than with medical and empirical psychologies, which tend to confine psychology to the positivistic manifestations of the nineteenth-century condition of the soul.

Archetypal psychology can be seen as a cultural movement, part of whose task is the re-visioning of psychology, psychopathology, and psychotherapy in terms of the Western cultural imagination. In an early review of the field and an examination of its main thrusts, Goldenberg (1975) regards archetypal psychology as a "third generation" derivative of the Jungian school in which Jung is recognized as the source but not the doctrine. Two themes of its directions, which she singles out – the emphasis upon psychopathology and the radical relativization and desubstantiation of the ego – will be discussed below.

It is without doubt that the first immediate father of archetypal psychology is Carl Gustav Jung, the Swiss psychologist (b. 1875; d. 1961). James Hillman, Rafael López-Pedraza, Patricia Berry, Paul Kugler, Murray Stein, Adolf Guggenbühl-Craig, Bianca Garufi, Robert Grinnell, and many others of the authors referred to below were trained as Jungian analysts. (However, a significant number of other authors mentioned – e.g., David L. Miller, Edward S. Casey, Gilbert Durand, Nor Hall, Mary Watkins, Robert Sardello – did not receive this specific Jungian formation and contribute to archetypal psychology from phenomenology, literature, poetry, philosophy, religious studies, etc.) From Jung comes the idea that the basic and universal structures of the psyche, the formal patterns of its relational modes, are archetypal patterns. These are like psychic organs, congenitally given with the psyche itself (yet not necessarily genetically inherited), even if somewhat modified by historical and geographical factors. These patterns or *archai* appear in the arts, religions, dreams, and social customs of all peoples, and they manifest spontaneously in mental disorders. For Jung, they are anthropological and cultural, and also spiritual in that they transcend the empirical world of time and place and, in fact, are in themselves not phenomenal. Archetypal psychology, in distinction to Jungian, considers the archetypal to be always phenomenal (Avens 1980), thus avoiding the Kantian idealism implied in Jung (de Voogd 1977).

The primary, and irreducible, language of these archetypal patterns is the metaphorical discourse of myths. These can therefore be understood as the most fundamental patterns of human existence. To study human nature at its most basic level, one must turn to culture (mythology, religion, art, architecture, epic, drama, ritual) where these patterns are portrayed. The full implication of this move away from biochemical, socio-historical, and personal-behavioristic bases for human nature toward the imaginative has been articulated by Hillman as "the poetic basis of mind." Support for the archetypal and psychological significance of myth, besides the work of Jung, comes from Ernst Cassirer, Karl Kerényi, Erich Neumann, Heinrich Zimmer, Gilbert Durand, Joseph Campbell, Ginette Paris, and David L. Miller.

The second immediate father of archetypal psychology is Henry Corbin (b. 1903; d. 1978), the French scholar, philosopher, and mystic, principally known for his interpretation of Islamic thought. From Corbin (1971–73) comes the idea that the *mundus archetypalis* (*'alam al-mithal*) is also the *mundus imaginalis*. It is a distinct field of imaginal realities requiring methods and perceptual faculties different from the spiritual world beyond it or the empirical world of usual sense perception and naive formulation. The *mundus imaginalis* offers an ontological mode of locating the archetypes of the psyche, as the fundamental structures of the imagination or as fundamentally imaginative phenomena that are transcendent to the world of sense in their *value* if not their appearance. Their value lies in their theophanic nature and in their virtuality or potentiality, which is always ontologically more than actuality and its limits. (As phenomena they must appear, though this appearance is to the imagination or in the imagination.) The *mundus imaginalis* provides for archetypes a valuative and cosmic grounding, when this is needed, different from such bases as biological instinct, eternal forms, numbers, linguistic and social transmission, biochemical reactions, and genetic coding.

But more important than the ontological placing of archetypal realities is the double move of Corbin: (*a*) that the fundamental nature of the archetype is accessible to imagination first and presents itself first as image, so that (*b*) the entire procedure of archetypal psychology as a method is imaginative. Its exposition must be rhetorical and poetic, its reasoning not logical, and its therapeutic aim neither social adaptation nor personalistic individualizing, but rather a work in service of restoration of the patient to imaginal realities. The aim of therapy is the development of a sense of soul, the middle ground of psychic realities, and the method of therapy is the cultivation of imagination.

In extending the tradition of Jung and Corbin forward, archetypal psychology has had to go back to their predecessors, particularly the Neoplatonic tradition via Vico and the Renaissance (Ficino), through Proclus and Plotinus, to Plato (*Phaedo, Phaedrus, Meno, Symposium, Timaeus*), and most anciently to Heraclitus. (Corbin's works on Avicenna, Ibn' Arabi, and Sohrawardi belong also in this tradition, as does the work of Kathleen Raine on William Blake and Thomas Taylor, the English translator of the main writings of Plato and the Neoplatonists.)

The elaboration of this tradition by Hillman in Eranos lectures and in articles (1973*a*), by Miller in seminars at Syracuse University, by

López-Pedraza at the University of Caracas, and by Moore's (1982) and Boer's (1980) work on Ficino gives a different cast to archetypal psychology when compared with Jung's. There, the background is more strongly German (Nietzsche, Schopenhauer, Carus, von Hartmann, Kant, Goethe, Eckhart, and Böhme), Christian, psychiatric, and Eastern. Archetypal psychology situates itself more comfortably *south* of the Alps.

Especially – this Neoplatonic tradition is thoroughly Western even if it is not empirical in method, rationalist in conception, or otherworldly spiritual in appeal. This tradition holds to the notion of soul as a first principle, placing this soul as a *tertium* between the perspectives of body (matter, nature, empirics) and of mind (spirit, logic, idea). Soul as *tertium*, the perspective *between* others and from which others may be viewed, has been described as Hermetic consciousness (López-Pedraza 1977), as *"esse in anima"* (Jung, *CW* 6: 66, 77), as the position of the *mundus imaginalis* by Corbin, and by Neoplatonic writers on the intermediaries or figures of the *metaxy*. Body, soul, spirit: this tripartite anthropology further separates archetypal psychology from the usual Western dualistic division, whose history goes back before Descartes to at least the ninth century (869: Eighth General Council at Constantinople), occurring also in the mediaeval ascension of Averroës's Aristotelianism over Avicenna's Platonism. Consequences of this dualistic division are still being felt in that the psyche has become indistinguishable from bodily life, on the one hand, or from the life of the spirit on the other. In the dualistic tradition, psyche never had its own logos. There could be no true psychology. A first methodologically consistent attempt to articulate one in a *philosophical* style belongs also within the perimeters of archetypal psychology (Christou 1963).

2

Image and Soul: The Poetic Basis of Mind

The datum with which archetypal psychology begins is the image. The image was identified with the psyche by Jung ("image *is* psyche," *CW* 13:75), a maxim that archetypal psychology has elaborated to mean that the soul is constituted of images, that the soul is primarily an imagining activity most natively and paradigmatically presented by the dream. For it is in the dream that the dreamer himself performs as one image among others and where it can legitimately be shown that the dreamer is in the image rather than the image in the dreamer.

The source of images – dream images, fantasy images, poetic images – is the self-generative activity of the soul itself. In archetypal psychology, the word "image" therefore does not refer to an afterimage, the result of sensations and perceptions; nor does "image" mean a mental construct that represents in symbolic form certain ideas and feelings it expresses. In fact, the image has no referent beyond itself, neither proprioceptive, external, nor semantic: "Images don't stand for anything" (Hillman 1978). They are the psyche itself in its imaginative visibility; as primary *datum*, image is irreducible. (The relation of image and "structure" has been discussed by Berry 1974 and by Kugler 1979*b*.)

Visibility, however, need not mean that an image must be visually seen. It does not have to have hallucinatory properties that confuse the act of perceiving images with imagining them. Nor do images have to be heard as in a poetic passage. Such notions of "visibility" tend to literalize images as distinct events presented to the senses. Hence Casey (1974), in his groundbreaking essay "Toward an Archetypal Imagination," states that an image is not what one sees, but the way in which one sees. An image is given by the imagining perspective and can only be perceived by an act of imagining.

The autochthonous quality of images as *independent* (Watkins 1981) of the subjective, perceiving imagination takes Casey's idea one step further. *First,* one believes images are hallucinations (things seen); *then* one recognizes them as acts of subjective imagining; but then, *third,* comes the awareness that images are independent of subjectivity and even of the imagination itself as a mental activity. Images come and go (as in dreams) at their own will, with their own rhythm, within their own fields of relations, undetermined by personal psychodynamics. In fact, images are the fundamentals that make the movements of psychodynamics possible. They claim reality, that is, authority, objectivity, and certitude. In this third recognition, the mind is in the imagination rather than the imagination in the mind. The noetic and the imaginal no longer oppose each other (Hillman 1981*a,b*). "Yet this is still 'psychology' although no longer science; it is psychology in the wider meaning of the word, a psychological activity of creative nature, in which creative fantasy is given prior place" (*CW*6: 84).

Corbin (1958) attributes this recognition to the awakened heart as *locus* of imagining, a *locus* also familiar in the Western tradition from Michelangelo's *l'immagine del cuor.* This interdependence of heart and image intimately ties the very basis of archetypal psychology with the phenomena of love (*q.v.* eros). Corbin's theory of creative imagination of the heart further implies for psychology that, when it bases itself in the image, it must at the same time recognize that imagination is not merely a human faculty but an activity of soul to which the human imagination bears witness. It is not we who imagine, but we who are imagined.

When "image" is thus transposed from a human representation of its conditions to a *sui generis* activity of soul in independent presentation of its bare nature, all empirical studies on imagination, dream, fantasy, and the creative process in artists, as well as methods of *rêve dirigé,* will contribute little to a psychology of the image if they start with the empirics of imagining rather than with the phenomenon of the image – which is not a product of imagining. Empirical approaches of analyzing and guiding images strive to gain control over them. Archetypal psychology distinguishes itself radically from these methods of image control as has been cogently argued by Watkins (1976, 1981). Casey's turning of the notion of image from something seen to a way of seeing (a seeing of the heart – Corbin) offers archetypal psychology's solution to an old dilemma between true (*vera*) imagination (Paracelsus) and false, or fancy (Coleridge). For archetypal psychology, the distinction depends upon the way in which the image is responded to and worked. The criteria it uses, therefore, refer to *response*: metaphorical and imaginative as being a better response than fanciful or literal and this because, where the former response is "fecund" (Langer), furthering the deepening and elaboration of the image, the latter responses dissipate or program the image into more naive, shallow, or fixedly dogmatic significance.

For archetypal psychology, images are neither good nor bad, true nor false, demonic nor angelic (Hillman 1977*a*), though an image always implicates "a precisely qualified context, mood and scene" (as Hillman 1977*b* has on one occasion defined the image). Thus they do invite judgment as a further precision of the image, judgment arising from the image itself as an effect of the image's own presentation of a claim for response. To suspend judgment, therefore, is to fall into the objectivist fantasy. Judgments are inherent to the image (as a work of art brings with it the standards by which it can be measured or a text brings with it the hermeneutics by which it can be interpreted). Archetypal psychology examines the judgments about the image imagistically, regarding them as its further specifications and as psychological statements not to be taken literally from a spiritual, purely noetic, vantage point detached from the context of the image judged.

The emphasis upon response has led archetypal psychology to use the analogy of the craftsman when discussing moral judgments. How well has the image worked; does the image release and refine further imagining? Does the response "stick to the image" (López-Pedraza) as the task at hand rather than associate or amplify into non-imagistic symbolisms, personal opinions, and interpretations? Such are the questions asked by archetypal psychology.

"Stick to the image" (cf. *CW* 16: 320) has become a golden rule of archetypal psychology's method, and this because the image is the primary psychological *datum*. Though the image always implies more than it presents, "the depth of the image – its limitless ambiguities ... can only be partly grasped as implications. To expand upon the dream image is also to narrow it – a further reason we wish never to stray too far from the source" (Berry 1974).

It must be noted that the "source" is *complex*: archetypal psychology is complex at the beginning, since the image is a self-limiting multiple relationship of meanings, moods, historical events, qualitative details, and expressive possibilities. As its referent is imaginal, it always retains a virtuality beyond its actuality (Corbin 1977). An image always seems more profound (archetypal), more powerful (potential), and more beautiful (theophanic) than the comprehension of it, hence the feeling, while recording a dream, of seeing through a glass darkly. Hence, too, the driving necessity in the arts, for they provide complicated disciplines that can actualize the complex virtuality of the image.

This polysemantic complexity bespeaks a polytheistic psychology of personifications analogous with Jung's theory of complexes as the multiple consciousness at the base of psychic life (*CW* 8: 388ff.). By starting with a complex datum – the image – archetypal psychology is saved from accounting for psychic life in simplistic terms of elementary mechanisms, primordialities of origins, or numerically limited basic structures. Reductionism is defeated from the start because the mind is poetic to begin with, and consciousness is not a later, secondary elaboration upon a primitive base, but is given with that base in each image.

The "poetic basis of mind" was a thesis Hillman (1975a) first set forth in his 1972 Terry Lectures at Yale University. It states that archetypal psychology "starts neither in the physiology of the brain, the structure of language, the organization of society, nor the analysis of behavior, but in processes of imagination." The inherent relation between psychology and the cultural imagination is necessitated by the nature of mind. The most fecund approach to the study of mind is thus through its highest imaginational responses (Hough 1973, Giegerich 1982, Berry 1982) where the images are most fully released and elaborated.

§ ≈ ≈ ≈ ≈ ≈ ≈ ≈ ≈ ≈ ≈ ≈ ≈

3

Archetypal Image

Archetypal psychology *axiomatically* assumes imagistic universals, comparable to the *universali fantastici* of Vico (*Scienza Nuova*, par. 381), that is, mythical figures that provide the poetic characteristics of human thought, feeling, and action, as well as the physiognomic intelligibility of the qualitative worlds of natural phenomena. By means of the archetypal image, natural phenomena present faces that speak to the imagining soul rather than only conceal hidden laws and probabilities and manifest their objectification.

A psychological universal must be considered *psychologically*. An archetypal image is psychologically "universal," because its effect amplifies and depersonalizes. Even if the notion of image regards each image as an individualized, unique event, as "that image there and no other," such an image is universal because it resonates with collective, trans-empirical importance. Thus, archetypal psychology uses "universal" as an adjective, declaring a substantive perduring *value*, which ontology states as a hypostasis. And, the universals problem for psychology is not whether they exist, where, and how they participate in particulars, but rather whether a personal individual event can be recognized as bearing essential and collective importance. Psychologically, the universals problem is presented by the soul itself whose perspective is harmoniously both the narrow particularity of felt experience and the universality of archetypally human experience. In Neoplatonic thought, soul could be spoken of as both my soul and world soul, and what was true of one was true of both. Thus, the universality of an archetypal image means also that the response to the image implies more than personal consequences, raising the soul itself beyond its egocentric confines (soul-making) and broadening the events of nature from discrete atomic particulars to aesthetic signatures bearing information for soul.

Because archetypal psychology gives priority to particular pattern over literal particle – and considers that particular events are always themselves imagistic and therefore ensouled – imagination too is assumed to be primordially patterned into typical themes, motifs, regions, genres, syndromes. These kinds of patterns inform all psychic life. Gilbert Durand (1960, 1979) – following upon the lines opened by Bachelard – and Durand's Centre de Recherche sur l'Imaginaire (*w3.u-grenoble3.fr/cri/*) have been charting the inherent organization of the imaginary as the basis of cultural anthropology and sociology, even as the basis of psychological meaning in all consciousness. Durand's papers published in the *Eranos Yearbooks* since 1964 present a range of archetypal cultural analysis.

Archetypal psychology has pressed beyond the collection of objective data and the correlation of images as verbal or visual symbols. If archetypal images are the fundamentals of fantasy, they are the means by which the world is imagined, and therefore they are the models by which all knowledge, all experiences whatsoever become possible: "Every psychic process is an image and an 'imagining,' otherwise no consciousness could exist…" (*CW* 11: 889). An archetypal image operates like the original meaning of idea (from Greek *eidos* and *eidolon*): not only "that which" one sees but also that "by means of which" one sees. The demonstration of archetypal images is therefore as much in the act of seeing as in the object seen, since the archetypal image appears in consciousness itself as the governing fantasy by means of which consciousness is possible to begin with. Gathering of data does less to demonstrate objectively the existence of archetypes than it does to demonstrate the fantasy of "objective data."

Furthermore, unlike Jung who radically distinguishes between noumenal archetype *per se* and phenomenal archetypal image, archetypal psychology rigorously refuses even to speculate about a nonpresented archetype *per se*. Its concern is with the phenomenon: the archetypal image. This leads to the next step: "… any image can be considered archetypal. The word 'archetypal' rather than pointing at something … points *to* something, and this is *value* … by archetypal psychology we mean a psychology of value. And our appellative move is aimed to restore psychology to its widest, richest, and deepest volume so that it would resonate with soul in its descriptions as unfathomable, multiple, prior, generative, and necessary. As all images can gain this archetypal sense, so all psychology can be archetypal ... 'Archetypal' here refers to a move one makes rather than to a thing that is" (Hillman 1977b).

Here, archetypal psychology "sees through" itself as strictly a psychology of archetypes, a mere analysis of structures of being (gods in their myths), and, by emphasizing the valuative function of the adjective *archetypal*, restores to images their primordial place as that which gives psychic value to the world. Any image termed *archetypal* is immediately valued as universal, trans-historical, basically profound, generative, highly intentional, and necessary.

Since "archetypal" connotes both intentional force (Jung's "instinct") and the mythical field of personifications (Hillman's "gods"), an archetypal image is animated like an animal (one of Hillman's frequent metaphors for images) and like a person whom one loves, fears, delights in, is inhibited by, and so forth. As intentional force and person, such an image presents a claim – moral, erotic, intellectual, aesthetic – and demands a response. It is an "affecting presence" (Armstrong 1971) offering an affective relationship. It seems to bear prior knowledge (coded information) and an instinctive direction for a destiny, as if prophetic, prognostic. Images in "dreams mean well for us, back us up and urge us on, understand us more deeply than we understand ourselves, expand our sensuousness and spirit, continually make up new things to give us – and this feeling of being loved by the images ... call it imaginal love" (Hillman 1979a). This message-bearing experience of the image – and the feeling of blessing that an image can bring – recalls the Neoplatonic sense of images as daimones and angels (message bearers). "Perhaps – who knows? – these eternal images are what men mean by fate" (CW7: 183).

Although an archetypal image presents itself as impacted with meaning, this is not given simply as revelation. It must be *made* through "image work" and "dream work" (Hillman 1977b, 1979a). The modes of this work may be concrete and physical as in art, movement, play, and occupational therapies; but more importantly (because less fixedly symbolic), this work is done by "sticking to the image" as a psychological penetration of what is actually presented including the stance of consciousness that is attempting the hermeneutic. Image work is not legitimately such unless the implicit involvement of a subjective perspective is admitted from the start, for it too is part of the image and in its fantasy.

Image work requires both aesthetic culture and a background in myths and symbols for appreciation of the universalities of images. This work also requires a series of tactical moves (Hillman and Berry 1977), frequently linguistic and phonetic (Sardello et al. 1978; Severson 1978; Kugler 1979b) and etymological (Lockhart 1978, 1980; Kugelmann 1983), and also grammatical and syntactical experimentation (Ritsema 1976; Hillman 1978a). Other tactical moves concerning emotion, texture, repetitions, reversals, and restatements have been described by Berry (1974).

The primary intention of this verbal work with images is the "recovery of soul in speech" (Sardello 1978a), which at the same time reveals the erotic and aesthetic aspect of images – that they captivate, charm, persuade, have a rhetorical effect on soul beyond their symbolic content. Image-work restores the original poetic sense to images, freeing them from serving a narrational context, having to tell a story with its linear, sequential, and causal implications that foster first-person reports of the egocentric actions and intentions of a personalistic subject. The distinction between image and narrative (Berry 1974; Miller 1976a) is fundamental to the distinction in imaginative style between archetypal polytheistic psychology and traditional psychologies that are egocentered, epic narrations (therapy).

Three further developments in theory of archetypal images are worth attention. Paul Kugler's work (1978, 1979a) elaborates an acoustic theory of images as structures of invariant meaning apart from linguistic, etymological, semantic, and syntactical meaning. Charles Boer and Peter Kugler (1977) have correlated archetypal images with the theory of perception of J.J. Gibson, asserting that archetypal images are afforded directly by the environment (and are not subjective), so that "archetypal psychology is mythical realism." Casey (1979) sets forth the idea that imagination is so closely related with time, both psychologically and ontologically, that actual image-work not only takes time into soul or makes temporal events soul events but also makes time in soul.

4

Soul

The primary metaphor of psychology must be soul. Psychology (*logos* of *psyche*) etymologically means: reason or speech or intelligible account of soul. It is psychology's job to find logos for psyche, to provide soul with an adequate account of itself. Psyche as the *anima mundi*, the Neoplatonic soul of the world, is already there with the world itself, so that a second task of psychology is to hear psyche speaking through all things of the world, thereby recovering the world as a place of soul (soul-making).

In its own speaking about the soul, archetypal psychology maintains an elusive obliqueness (Romanyshyn 1978–79). This continual carefulness not to substantiate soul follows this maxim: "By soul I mean, first of all, a perspective rather than a substance, a viewpoint toward things rather than a thing itself" (Hillman 1975a). In a long examination of "soul," Hillman (1964) concludes: "The soul is a deliberately ambiguous concept resisting all definition in the same manner as do all ultimate symbols that provide the root metaphors for the systems of human thought." In this same passage, a circumscription of the term states: "We are not able to use the word in an unambiguous way, even though we take it to refer to that unknown human factor that makes meaning possible, turns events into experiences, and is communicated in love." In 1967a, a fourth aspect was added: the soul has a religious concern. And in 1975a, three further qualifications were adjoined: "First, 'soul' refers to the *deepening* of events into experiences; second, the significance soul makes possible, whether in love or religious concern, derives from its *special relation with death*. And third, by 'soul' I mean the imaginative possibility in our natures, the experiencing through reflective speculation, dream, image, and *fantasy* – that mode, which recognizes all realities as primarily symbolic or metaphorical."

The literalizing and ontologizing dangers attendant upon the ele-
vation of soul to first principle are met by a certain subversive tone in
archetypal psychology that speaks of soul events in imagistic, ironic,
and even humorous ways (Hillman and Berry 1977). Common to many
writers, though different in each – Guggenbühl-Craig, Miller, Ziegler,
López-Pedraza, Giegerich, Sardello – is this dark and mordant style.
Psyche is kept close to its shadows. There is a continual attempt to
break the vessels even as they are being formed.

The term "soul" is also used freely without defining specific usages and
senses in order to keep present its full connotative power. And it is used
interchangeably with the Greek *psyche*, the Greek mythic figure Psyche
(Apuleius' tale of *Amor and Psyche*), the Germanic *Seele*, and the Latin *anima*.
Here, "anima" in the more specific Jungian description as a personified
figure and function of the imagination (E. Jung 1957; Hillman 1973c,
1974b) bestows rich imagery, pathologies, and feeling qualities to what
otherwise might become only a philosophical concept.

The human being is set within the field of soul; soul is the metaphor
that includes the human. "*Dasein* as *esse in anima* infinitely surpasses
man" (Avens 1982a). Even if human life is only one manifestation of
the psyche, a human life is always a psychological life – which is how
archetypal psychology reads the Aristotelian notion of soul as life and
the Christian doctrine of the soul as immortal, i.e., beyond the confines
of individual limitation. A humanistic or personalistic psychology will
always fail the full perspective of soul that extends beyond human,
personal behavior. This move, which places man within psyche (rather
than psyche within man), revisions all human activity whatsoever as
psychological. Every piece of human behavior, whatever its manifest
and literal content, is always also a psychological statement.

If every statement has psychological content, then every statement
may be scrutinized for its psychological significance, for what it means
to soul. Speech about soul itself – what it is, its body relations, its origins
and development, what it consists in, how it functions – are psychology's concern only because these are the enduring ways the soul gives
accounts of itself in conceptual form. They belong to its *soul-making*,
its ongoing fantasy activity, and these accounts called "psychology"
ought to be taken fictionally rather than only as positivistic answers

about the nature of the soul. The soul can be an object of study only when it is also recognized as the subject studying itself by means of the fictions and metaphors of objectivity. This scrutiny of statements for their psychic implications is a strategical principle of archetypal psychology, providing its tactical method called "psychologizing, or seeing through" (Hillman 1975a). The method puts into practice the notion of the unconscious: whatever is stated contains an unconsciousness within the statement. "Unconscious" takes on the meaning of implication and supposition (Berry 1974), that is, what is folded in or held beneath. Statements from any field whatsoever thus become psychological, or revelations of psyche, when their literalism is subverted to allow their suppositions to appear. The strategy implies that psychology cannot be limited to being one field among others since psyche itself permeates all fields and things of the world.

Anima and Rhetoric

By speaking of soul as a primary *metaphor*, rather than defining soul substantively and attempting to derive its ontological status from empirical demonstration or theological (metaphysical) argument, archetypal psychology recognizes that psychic reality is inextricably involved with *rhetoric*. The perspective of soul is inseparable from the manner of speaking of soul, a manner that evokes soul, brings it to life, and persuades us into a psychological perspective. In its concern with rhetoric, archetypal psychology has relied on literary and poetic devices to expound its vision, all the while working at "seeing through" the mechanistic and personalistic metaphors employed by other psychologies so as to recover soul from those literalisms. The polemical foray into others' preserves is necessary to the rhetorical mode.

Soul and Myth

The primary rhetoric of archetypal psychology is myth. Here, the path had already been pioneered by Freud, Jung, and Cassirer (Avens 1980), and, of course, by a tradition of mythical thinking going back through the Romantics and Vico to Plato. This move toward mythical accounts as a psychological language locates psychology in the cultural imagination. Secondly, these myths are themselves metaphors (or, as Vico said "metaphor…is a myth [*fabula*] in brief" [*Scienza Nuova*, par. 404]), so that by relying on myths as its primary rhetoric, archetypal psychology grounds itself in a fantasy that cannot be taken historically, physically, literally. Even if the recollection of mythology is perhaps the single most characteristic move shared by all "archetypalists," the myths themselves are understood as metaphors – never as transcendental metaphysics whose categories are divine figures. "Myths do not ground, they open" (Hillman 1979*a*). The role of myth in archetypal psychology is not to provide an exhaustive catalogue of possible behaviors or to circumscribe the forms of transpersonal energies (in the Neoplatonic sense), but rather to open the questions of life to transpersonal and culturally imaginative reflection. We may thereby see our ordinary lives embedded in and ennobled by the dramatic and world-creative life of mythical figures (Bedford 1981). The study of mythology allows events to be recognized against their mythical background. More important, however, is that the study of mythology enables one to perceive and experience the life of the soul mythically.

5

Soul, Metaphor, and Fantasy

The philosophical problem "how to define soul" or how to state a "logos of soul" (Christou 1963) must be viewed in the first place as a psychological phenomenon, one that arises from the soul's own desire for self-knowledge, which can best be satisfied in terms of its own constitution: images. Thus the logos of soul, i.e., a true speaking of it, will be in an imagistic style, an account or *recit* (Corbin 1979) that is through and through metaphorical.

The statement above that "the primary metaphor of psychology must be soul" attempts two things: (*a*) to state the soul's nature in its own language (metaphor) and (*b*) to recognize that all statements in psychology about soul are metaphors. In this way, soul-as-metaphor leads beyond the problem of "how to define soul" and encourages an account of the soul toward imagining itself rather than defining itself. Here, metaphor serves a psychological function: it becomes an instrument of soul-making rather than a mere "figure of speech" because it transposes the soul's questioning about its nature to a mythopoesis of actual imagining, an ongoing psychological creation (Berry 1982).

Soul-as-metaphor also describes how the soul acts. It performs as does a metaphor, transposing meaning and releasing interior, buried significance. Whatever is heard with the ear of soul reverberates with under- and overtones (Moore 1978). The perspective darkens with a deeper light. But this metaphorical perspective also kills: it brings about the death of naive realism, naturalism, and literal understanding. The relation of soul to death – a theme running all through archetypal psychology – is thus a function of the psyche's metaphorical activity. The metaphorical mode does not speak in declarative statements or explain in clear contrasts. It delivers all things to their shadows. Its perspective defeats any heroic attempt to gain a firm grip on phenomena; instead, the metaphorical mode of soul is "elusive, allusive, illusive" (Romanyshyn 1977), undermining the very definition of consciousness as intentionality and its history as development.

Human awareness fails in its comprehension not because of original sin or personal neurosis or because of the obstinacy of the objective world to which it is supposedly opposed. Human awareness fails, according to a psychology based on soul, because the soul's metaphorical nature has a suicidal necessity (Hillman 1964), an underworld affiliation (Hillman 1979a), a "morbism" (Ziegler 1980), a destiny – different from day-world claims – which makes the psyche fundamentally unable to submit to the *hubris* of an egocentric notion of subjectivity as achievement (*Leistung*), defined as cognition, conation, intention, perception, and so forth.

Thus, that sense of weakness (López-Pedraza 1977, 1982), inferiority (Hillman 1977c), mortification (Berry 1973), masochism (Cowan 1979), darkness (Winquist 1981), and failure (Hillman 1972b) is inherent to the *mode* of metaphor itself, which defeats conscious understanding as a control over phenomena. Metaphor, as the soul's *mode* of logos, ultimately results in that abandonment to the given that approximates mysticism (Avens 1980).

The metaphorical transposition – this "death-dealing" move that at the same time re-awakens consciousness to a sense of soul – is at the heart of archetypal psychology's mission, its world intention. As Freud and Jung both attempted to discover the fundamental "mistake" in Western culture so as to resolve the misery of man trapped in the decline of the West, so archetypal psychology specifies this mistake as loss of soul, which it further identifies with loss of images and the imaginal sense. The result has been an intensification of subjectivity (Durand 1975), showing both in the self-enclosed egocentricity and the hyperactivism, or life-fanaticism, of Western (rather, Northern) consciousness that has lost its relation with death and the underworld.

That re-imagining and re-animating of the cultural psyche to which archetypal psychology aspires necessitates pathologizing, for only this weakening or "falling apart" (Hillman 1975a) breaks through self-enclosed subjectivity and restores it to its depth in soul, allowing soul to reappear again in the world of things.

The re-animation of things by means of metaphor was already indicated by Vico (*Scienza Nuova*, par. 186) who wrote that "metaphor... gives sense and passion to insensate things." As the metaphorical perspective gives new animation to soul, so too it re-vitalizes areas that had been assumed not ensouled and not psychological: the events of the body and medicine, the ecological world, the man-made phenomena of architecture and transportation, education, food, bureaucratic language and systems. These have all been examined as metaphorical images and have become subject to intense psychological revision by Sardello and his students first at the University of Dallas and subsequently at the Dallas Institute of Humanities and Culture (Thomas, Stroud, Moore). The metaphorical perspective, which revisions worldly phenomena as images, can find "sense and passion" where the Cartesian mind sees the mere extension of de-souled insensate objects. In this way, the poetic basis of mind takes psychology out of the confines of laboratory and consulting room, and even beyond the personal subjectivity of the human person, into a psychology of things as objectifications of images with interiority, things as the display of fantasy.

For archetypal psychology, "fantasy" and "reality" change places and values. First, they are no longer opposed. Second, fantasy is never merely mentally subjective, but is always being enacted and embodied (Hillman 1972a). Third, whatever is physically or literally "real" is always also a fantasy image. Thus the world of so-called hard factual reality is always also the display of a specifically shaped fantasy, as if to say, along with Wallace Stevens, the American philosopher-poet of imagination on whom archetypal psychology often draws, there is always "a poem at the heart of things." Jung stated the same idea (*CW* 6: 18): "The psyche creates reality everyday. The only expression I can say for this activity is *fantasy*." And he takes the word *fantasy* "from poetic usage" (*CW* 6:743).

The latest explorations of archetypal psychology – some published in *Spring: An Annual of Archetypal Psychology and Jungian Thought* (1979– 82) – have been in the direction of poetics, aesthetics, and literary criticism. This is less the influence of contemporary psychoanalytic concerns with language than it is the re-appraisal of psychology itself as an activity of *poesis* and the fact that fantasy is the archetypal activity of the psyche.

6

Soul and Spirit

If imagining is the native activity of the *anima mundi*, then fantasy is always going on and is not subject to a phenomenological *epoché* (Husserl; setting aside or bracketing out in order to move directly to the event itself). Moreover, if fantasy is always going on, then *epoché* is itself a fantasy: of isolating, of objectification, and of a consciousness that can be truly addressed by phenomena as they are. Archetypal psychology maintains, however, that we can never be purely phenomenal or truly objective. One is never beyond the subjectivism given with the soul's native dominants of fantasy structures. These dominate subjective perspectives and organize them into "stances," so that the only objectivity that could be approximated results from the subjective eye turned in on itself, regarding its own regard, examining its own perspective for the archetypal subjects (*q.v.* personifying) who are at this moment governing our way of being in the world among phenomena. Psychology as an objective science is forever impossible once one has recognized that objectivity is itself a poetic genre (similar to "writer-as-mirror" in French naturalism), a mode that constructs the world so that things appear as sheer things (not faces, not animated, not with interiority), subject to will, separate from each other, mute, without sense, or passion.

One position is particularly obdurate in yielding to the fantasy that fantasy is always going on, and that is the stance of spirit. It appears as scientific objectivity, as metaphysics, and as theology. And where archetypal psychology has attacked these approaches, it is part of a wider strategy to distinguish the methods and rhetoric of soul from those of spirit, so that soul is not forced to forfeit its style to fulfill the obligations required by a spiritual perspective, whether philosophical, scientific, or religious. For psychology to be possible at all it must keep the distinction between soul and spirit (Hillman 1976, 1975*a*, 1977*a*).

At times, the spirit position with its rhetoric of order, number, knowledge, permanency, and self-defensive logic has been discussed as "senex" and Saturnian (Vitale 1973; Hillman 1975d); at other times, because of its rhetoric of clarity and detached observation, it has been discussed as Apollonic (Hillman 1972c); on other occasions, because of the rhetoric of unity, ultimacy, identity, it has been termed "monotheistic"; and in yet other contexts, "heroic" and also "puer" (Hillman 1967b).

While recognizing that the spirit perspective must place itself above (as the soul places itself as inferior) and speak in transcendent, ultimate, and pure terms, archetypal psychology conceives its task to be one of imagining the spirit language of "truth," "faith," "law," and the like as a rhetoric of spirit, even if spirit is obliged by this same rhetoric to take its stance truthfully and faithfully, i.e., literally.

The distinction between soul and spirit further guards against psychological therapy becoming confused with spiritual disciplines – whether Eastern or Western – and gives yet another reason for archetypal psychology to eschew borrowings from meditative techniques and/or operant conditioning, both of which conceptualize psychic events in spiritual terms.

7

Soul-Making

The underlying aspiration of its work archetypal psychology has called "soul-making," taking the phrase from the poets William Blake and, particularly, John Keats: "Call the world if you please, 'The vale of Soul-making.' Then you will find out the use of the world…" For all its emphasis upon the individualized soul, archetypal psychology sets this soul, and its making, squarely in the midst of the world. And, it does not seek a way out of or beyond the world toward redemption or mystical transcendence, because "the way through the world is more difficult to find than the way beyond it" (Wallace Stevens, "Reply to Papini"). The curative or salvational vision of archetypal psychology focuses upon the soul in the world, which is also the soul of the world (*anima mundi*). The idea of soul-making by taking any world event as also a place of soul insists that even this Neoplatonic and "arcane" psychology is nonetheless embedded in the "vale" and its engagement therein. The artificial tension between soul and world, private and public, interior and exterior thus disappears when the soul as *anima mundi*, and its making, is located in the world.

More specifically, the act of soul-making is imagining, since images are the psyche, its stuff, and its perspective. Crafting images – such as discussed below in regard to therapy – is thus an equivalent of soul-making. This crafting can take place in the concrete modes of the artisan, a work of the hands, and with the morality of the hands. And, it can take place in sophisticated elaborations of reflection, religion, relationships, social action, so long as these activities are imagined from the perspective of soul, soul as uppermost concern.

In other words, only when imagination is recognized as an engagement at the borders of the human and a work in relation with mythic dominants can this articulation of images be considered a psycho-poesis

(Miller 1976b), or soul-making. Its intention is the realization of the images – for they are the psyche – and not merely of the human subject. As Corbin has said: "It is their individuation, not ours," suggesting that soul-making can be most succinctly defined as the individuation of imaginal reality.

Soul-making is also described as imaging, that is, seeing or hearing by means of an imagining that sees through an event to its image. Imaging means releasing events from their literal understanding into a mythical appreciation. Soul-making, in this sense, is equated with de-literalizing – that psychological attitude that suspiciously disallows the naive and given level of events in order to search out their shadowy, metaphorical significances for soul.

So the question of soul-making is "what does this event, this thing, this moment move in my soul? What does it mean to my death?" The question of death enters because it is in regard to death that the perspective of soul is distinguished most starkly from the perspective of natural life.

Soul-making does imply a metaphysical fantasy, and the implied metaphysics of archetypal psychology are best found in *The Dream and the Underworld* (Hillman 1979a), which elaborates the relations between psyche and death. There the dream is taken as the paradigm of the psyche – where the psyche presents itself encompassing the ego and engaged in its own work (dream-work). From the dream, one may assume that the psyche is fundamentally concerned with its imaginings and only secondarily concerned with subjective experiences in the day-world which the dream transforms into images, i.e., into soul. The dream is thus making soul each night. Images become the means of translating life-events into soul, and this work, aided by the conscious elaboration of imagination, builds an imaginal vessel, or "ship of death" (a phrase taken from D.H. Lawrence), that is similar to the subtle body, or *ochema* of the Neoplatonists (cf. Avens 1982b).

The question of the soul's immortality is not directly answered by a metaphysical statement. Rather, the very nature of the soul in the dream – or at least the perspective of soul toward the dream – shows its inattention to and disregard for mortal experience as such, even for physical death itself, receiving into its purview only those faces and events from the mortal world that bear upon the opus of its destiny.

8

Depth and the Vertical Direction

Since its beginning in Freud's study of the deep layers of the mind – pre-, sub-, or unconscious – the field of "depth psychology" (so named at the turn of the century by the Zurich psychiatrist Eugen Bleuler) has always been directed downward, whether toward buried memories of childhood or toward archaic mythologems. Archetypal psychology has taken this depth metaphor equally seriously – though less literally. It has carried the metaphor of depth of soul back in history to Heraclitus (Diels-Kranz, Frag. 45: *bathun*) and then to Augustine's *thesaurus* or *memoria* (*Confessions* X). Moreover, it has reverted Freud's own move into depth, the descent into the dream as described in his *Traumdeutung*, to the mythologies of the Underworld, Hades, Persephone, Dionysus – and to Christian theologies of descent (Miller 1981*b*) – exploring the fundamental relation of the psyche with the realm of the dead, which is also the realm of images or *eidola* (Hillman 1979*a*).

Because of the vertical direction of depth psychology, it is obliged to be concerned with depression and with the reduction of phenomena to their "deadly" essence, their pathologized extremity (Berry 1973), where we experience them as both materially destructive and negative and yet as the ground of support (Berry 1978*b*).

The literalization of downwardness in depth psychology has resulted in a narrowness of meaning: introverted inwardness within the person, into the "abyss" and "secret chamber" of the personal self (Augustine). What then of the relationship with others, with the horizontal world?

For archetypal psychology, the vertical direction refers to interiority as a capacity within all things. All things have an archetypal significance and are available to psychological penetration, and this interiority is manifested by the physiognomic character of the things of the horizontal world.

Depth is therefore not literally hidden, deep down, inside. Rather, the fantasy of depth encourages us to look at the world again, to read each event for "something deeper," to "insearch" (Hillman 1967a) rather than to research, for yet further significance below what seems merely evident and natural. The downward interiorizing fantasy is thus at the very basis of all psychoanalysis. The fantasy of hidden depths ensouls the world and fosters imagining ever deeper into things. Depth – rather than a literal or physical location – is a primary metaphor necessary for psychological thinking (or "psychologizing," Hillman 1975a).

9

Cultural Locus: North and South

The downward direction may also be envisioned as Southward. Unlike the main psychologies of the twentieth century, which have drawn their sources from Northern Europe (the German language and the Protestant-Jewish monotheistic *Weltanschauung*), archetypal psychology starts in the South. Neither Greek nor Renaissance civilization developed "psychologies" as such. The word "psychology" and most modern psychological terms (Hillman 1972c) do not appear in an active sense until the nineteenth century. In recognition of these historical facts, archetypal psychology situates its work in a pre-psychological geography, where the culture of imagination and the modes of living carried what had to be formulated in the North as "psychology." "Psychology" is a necessity of a post-reformational culture that had been deprived of its poetic base.

Since, as Casey (1982) maintains, place is prior to the possibility of thought – all thought must be placed in order to be – archetypal psychology requires an imaginal location. Freud's "Vienna" and Jung's "Zurich," or the "California Schools" are fantasy locations, not merely sociological and historical contexts. They place the ideas in a geographical image. Such is "south" in the imagination of archetypal psychology.

"South" is both an ethnic, cultural, geographic place and a symbolic one. It is both the Mediterranean culture, its images and textual sources, its sensual and concrete humanity, its gods and goddesses and their myths, its tragic and picaresque genres (rather than the epic heroism of the North); and it is a symbolic stance "below the border," which does not view that region of the soul only from a northern moralistic perspective. The unconscious thus becomes radically re-visioned and may as well be located "up north" (as Aryan, Apollonic, Germanic, positivistic, voluntaristic, rationalistic, Cartesian, protestant, scientistic, personalistic, monotheistic, etc.). Even the family, rather than a source of "northern" neurosis, can be revalued as the ground of ancestral and societal binding.

By remembering this fundamental division in Western cultural history, archetypal psychology eludes the conventional dilemma of "East and West." Positions usually given over to the "East" are included within archetypal psychology's own orientation. Having re-oriented consciousness toward non-ego factors – the multiple personifications of the soul, the elaboration of the imaginal ground of myths, the direct immediacy of sense experience coupled with the ambiguity of its interpretation, and the radically relative phenomenality of the "ego" itself as but one fantasy of the psyche – archetypal psychology makes superfluous the move toward oriental disciplines, which have had to be found in the East, when psychology is identified with the perspectives of northern psychic geography.

Roberts Avens's monographs (1980, 1982a,b) show that archetypal psychology is nothing less than a parallel formulation of certain Eastern philosophies. Like them, it too dissolves ego, ontology, substantiality, literalisms of self and divisions between it and things – the entire conceptual apparatus, which northern psychology constructs from the heroic ego and in its defense – into the psychic reality of imagination experienced in immediacy. The "emptying out" of Western positivism comparable to a Zen exercise or a way of Nirvana, is precisely what archetypal psychology has effectuated, though by means that are utterly Western, where "Western" refers to a psychology of soul as imagined in the tradition of the South.

10

Polytheistic Psychology and Religion

Of all the moves, none is so far-reaching in cultural implication as the attempt to recover the perspectives of polytheism. Moore (1980) considers this perspective to be the rational consequent of a psychology based in anima that can "animate" the study of religion by offering both "a way of understanding religion ... and a way of going about religious studies." Miller's christology (1981a) demonstrates the relevance of the polytheistic perspective for even a religion whose dogma historically derives from an anti-polytheistic position. The complex issues of the new polytheism have been treated by Miller (1974, with an appendix by Hillman 1981) and by Goldenberg (1979). The polytheistic moves of archetypal psychology occur in four interrelated modes.

(1) The most accurate model of human existence will be able to account for its innate diversity, both among individuals and within each individual. Yet, this same model must also provide fundamental structures and values for this diversity. For both Freud and Jung, multiplicity is basic to human nature, and their models of man rely upon a polycentric fantasy. Freud's notion of the child as sexually polymorphous originates the libido in a polymorphic, polyvalent, and polycentric field of erogenous zones. Jung's model of personality is essentially multiple, and Jung correlates the plurality of its archetypal structure with the polytheistic stage of culture (CW 9.2: 427). Hence, "the soul's inherent multiplicity demands a theological fantasy of equal differentiation" (Hillman 1975a).

(2) The tradition of thought (Greek, Renaissance, Romantic) to which archetypal psychology claims it is an heir is set in polytheistic attitudes. The imaginative products of these historical periods cannot contribute further to psychology unless the consciousness that would

receive from them is able to transpose itself into a similar polytheistic framework. The high achievements of Western culture from which contemporary culture may find sources for its survival remain closed to modern consciousness unless it gains a perspective mimetic to what it is examining. Hence, polytheistic psychology is necessary for the continuity of culture.

(3) The social, political, and psychiatric critique implied throughout archetypal psychology mainly concerns the monotheistic hero myth (now called ego-psychology) of secular humanism, i.e., the single-centered, self-identified notion of subjective consciousness of humanism (from Protagoras to Sartre). It is this myth that has dominated the soul and leads to both unreflected action and self-blindness (Oedipus). It is responsible also for the repression of a psychological diversity that then appears as psychopathology. Hence, a polytheistic psychology is necessary for reawakening reflective consciousness and bringing a new reflection to psychopathology.

(4) The *perspectivalism* of archetypal psychology requires a deepening of subjectivity beyond mere Nietzschean perspectives or existential stances. Perspectives are *forms* of vision, rhetoric, values, epistemology, and lived styles that perdure independently of empirical individuality. For archetypal psychology, pluralism and multiplicity and relativism are not enough: these are merely philosophical generalities. Psychology needs to specify and differentiate each event, which it can do against the variegated background of archetypal configurations, or what polytheism called gods, in order to make multiplicity both authentic and precise. Thus the question it asks of an event is not *why* or *how*, but rather *what* specifically is being presented and ultimately *who*, which divine figure, is speaking in this style of consciousness, this form of presentation. Hence, a polytheistic psychology is necessary for the authorization of "a pluralistic universe" (William James 1909), for consistencies within it, and for precision of its differentiation.

The polytheistic analogy is both religious and not religious (Miller 1972, 1974; Bregman 1980; Scott 1980; Avens 1980). The gods are taken essentially, as foundations, so that psychology points beyond soul and can never be merely agnostic. The sacred and sacrificial dimension – the religious instinct as Jung calls it – is given a place of main value; and, in truth, it is precisely because of the appeal to the gods that value enters the psychological field, creating claims on each human life and giving personal acts more than personal significance. The gods are therefore the gods of religion and not mere *nomina*, categories, devices *ex machina*. They are respected as powers and persons and creators of value.

A distinction is nonetheless maintained between polytheism as psychology and as religion. This distinction is difficult because "depth analysis leads to the soul, which inevitably involves analysis in religion and even in theology, while at the same time living religion, experienced religion, originates in the human psyche and is as such a psychological phenomenon" (Hillman 1967a). When soul is the first metaphor, then psychology and religion must be intertwined and their distinction arbitrary or ambiguous. The question of polytheism is posed by the soul itself as soon as its perspective experiences the world as animated and its own nature as replete with changing diversity. That is, as soon as the soul is freed from ego domination, the question of polytheism arises.

Yet archetypal psychology is "not out to worship Greek gods or those of any other polytheistic high culture … We are not reviving a dead faith. For we are not concerned with faith" (Hillman 1975a; cf. A.H. Armstrong 1981). The gods of psychology are not believed in, not taken literally, not imagined theologically. "Religion approaches gods with ritual, prayer, sacrifice, worship, creed … In archetypal psychology, gods are *imagined*. They are approached through psychological methods of personifying, pathologizing, and psychologizing. They are formulated ambiguously, as metaphors for modes of experience and as numinous borderline persons. They are cosmic perspectives in which the soul participates" (ibid.). Mainly, the mode of this participation is reflection: the gods are discovered in recognizing the stance of one's perspective, one's psychological sensitivity to the configurations that dominate one's styles of thought and life. Gods for psychology do not have to be experienced in direct mystical encounter or in effigies, whether as concrete figures or as theological definitions.

A saying attributed to Hegel declares: "What is required is a monotheism of reason and heart, a polytheism of imagination and art" (Cook 1973). Inasmuch as archetypal psychology is imaginative, it requires imaginative first principles and polytheism becomes necessary, although it definitely does not carry on the rationalist separation between heart and art, between valuative and aesthetic sensitivities.

The critique of theological religion continues that done by Freud and Jung, though with an even more radical cast. Archetypal psychology does not attempt to correct the Judeo-Christian religion as illusion (Freud) or transform it as one-sided (Jung). It shifts the ground of the entire question to a polytheistic position. In this single stroke, it carries out Freud's and Jung's critiques to their ultimate consequent – the death of God as a monotheistic fantasy, while at the same time restoring the fullness of the gods in all things and, let it be said, reverting psychology itself to the recognition that it too is a religious activity (Hillman 1975a). If a religious instinct is inherent to the psyche as Jung maintained, then any psychology attempting to do justice to the psyche must recognize its religious nature.

A polytheistic vision differs from undifferentiated pantheism, holy vitalism, and naturalistic animism – which from the standpoint of monotheistic consciousness tend to be bunched together as "pagan" and "primitive." Gods in archetypal psychology are not some primal energy suffused through the universe nor are they imagined to be independent magical powers working on us through things. Gods are imagined as the formal intelligibility of the phenomenal world, allowing each thing to be discerned for its inherent intelligibility and for its specific place of belonging to this or that *kosmos* (ordered pattern or arrangement). The gods are places, and myths make place for psychic events that in an only human world become pathological. By offering shelter and altar, the gods can order and make intelligible the entire phenomenal world of nature and human consciousness. All phenomena are "saved" by the act of placing them, which at once gives them value. We discover what belongs where by means of likeness, the analogy of events with mythical configurations. This mode was current during millennia of our culture in alchemy, planetary astrology, natural philosophy, and medicine, each of which studied the microcosmic things in rapport with macrocosmic gods (Moore 1982; Boer 1980). It was this question of *placing* that was addressed to the Greek oracles: "To what gods or hero must I pray or sacrifice to achieve such and such a purpose?" If one knows where an event belongs, to whom it can be related, then one is able to proceed.

Today, however, the discovery of what belongs where, the *epistrophé* or reversion through likeness of an event to its mythical pattern, is less the aim of archetypal psychology than is an archetypal sensitivity that all things belong to myth. The study of these archetypal placings, deriving from the work of Frances Yates (1966) in regard to the Memory Theatre of the Florentine Giulio Camillo (b. 1480; d. 1544), has been carried out in some detail in seminars by López-Pedraza and Sardello.

11

Psychopathology

T he point of departure for the re-visioning of psychopathology is a statement from Jung (*CW* 13: 54): "The gods have become diseases; Zeus no longer rules Olympus but rather the solar plexus, and produces curious specimens for the doctor's consulting room..."

The link between gods and diseases is double: on the one hand, giving the dignity of archetypal significance and divine reflection to every symptom whatsoever, and on the other hand, suggesting that myth and its figures may be examined for patterns of pathology. Hillman (1974*a*) has called this pathology in mythical figures the *infirmitas* of the archetype, by which is meant both the essential "infirmity" of all archetypal forms – that they are not perfect, not transcendent, not idealizations – and that they therefore provide "nursing" to human conditions; they are the embracing backgrounds within which our personal sufferings can find support and be cared for.

The double link – that pathology is mythologized and mythology is pathologized – had already been adumbrated by Freud's presentation of the Oedipus myth as the key to the pathology of neurosis and even of the civilization as a whole. Before Freud, the link between *mythos* and *pathos* can be discovered in Nietzsche's *The Birth of Tragedy* and in the scholarly research of the great German classicist and encyclopedist W.H. Roscher, whose *Ephialtes* (1900), a monograph on Pan and the nightmare, was subtitled "A Mythopathological Study" (cf. Hillman 1972*a*).

The relations between myths and psychopathology are elaborated in a series of studies: López-Pedraza (1977) on Hermes and (1982) on the Titans; Berry (1975) on Demeter/Persephone and (1979*b*) on Echo; Moore (1979*a*) on Artemis; Micklem (1979) on Medusa; Hillman (1970*a*, 1975*d*) on Saturn, (1974*a*) on Athene and Ananke, (1972*c*) on Eros and Dionysus,

(1972*a*) on Pan, and (1967*b*) on the *puer eternus* or divinely youthful figure in various mythologies; M. Stein (1973) on Hephaistos and (1977) on Hera. In these studies, the myth is examined for its pathological implications. The hermeneutic begins with myths and mythical figures (not with a case), reading them downward for psychological understanding of the fantasies going on in behavior.

Archetypal psychology thereby follows the epistrophic (reversion) method of Corbin, returning to the higher principle in order to find place for and understand the lesser – the images before their examples. Imagination becomes a method for investigating and comprehending psychopathology. This hermeneutic method is also essentially Neoplatonic; it is the preferred way for deciphering the grotesque and pathologized configurations of Renaissance psychology. As Wind says in his "Observation on Method" (1967): "The commonplace may be understood as a reduction of the exceptional, but the exceptional cannot be understood by amplifying the commonplace. Both logically and causally the exceptional is crucial, because it introduces ... the more comprehensive category."

Precisely because myth presents the exceptional, the outlandish, and more-than-human dimension, it offers background to the sufferings of souls *in extremis*, i.e., what nineteenth-century medicine calls "psychopathology." The double movement between pathology and mythology moreover implies that the pathological is always going on in human life inasmuch as life enacts mythical fantasies. Archetypal psychology further claims that it is mainly through the wounds in human life that the gods enter (rather than through pronouncedly sacred or mystical events), because pathology is the most palpable manner of bearing witness to the powers beyond ego control and the insufficiency of the ego perspective.

This perpetually recurring "pathologizing" is defined as "the psyche's autonomous ability to create illness, morbidity, disorder, abnormality, and suffering in any aspect of its behavior and to experience and imagine life through this deformed and afflicted perspective" (Hillman 1975*a*). There is no cure of pathologizing; there is, instead, a re-evaluation.

That pathologizing is also a "deformed perspective" accounts for its place in the work of imagination that, according to Gaston Bachelard

(b. 1884; d. 1962) – another major source of the archetypal tradition – must proceed by "deforming the images offered by perception" (Bachelard 1943). It is this pathologized eye that, like that of the artist and the psychoanalyst, prevents the phenomena of the soul from being naively understood as merely natural. Following Jung (and his research into alchemy), psychological work is an *opus contra naturam*. This idea Hillman (1975a) follows further by attacking the "naturalistic fallacy," which dominates most normative psychologies.

Another direction of the *mythos/pathos* connection starts with one specific form of pathology, searching it for its mythical possibilities, as if to uncover "the God in the disease." Examples are: Lockhart (1977), cancer; Moore (1979b), asthma; Leveranz (1979), epilepsy; Hawkins (1979), migraine; Severson (1979), skin disorders; Kugelmann, glaucoma; Sipiora (1981), tuberculosis.

There are also more general reflections upon pathology revisioned within an archetypal hermeneutic: R. Stein (1974) on psychosexual disorders; Guggenbühl-Craig (1971) on the archetypal power problem in medical attitudes; Ziegler (1980) on archetypal medicine; Sardello (1980a) on medicine, disease, and the body. These works look at the body, pathology, and its treatment altogether free from the positivism of the clinical and empirical traditions that have come down to the twentieth century from nineteenth-century scientistic, materialistic medicine, its views of health, disease, and the power-hero role of the physician.

In one respect, the position here is close to the anti-psychiatry of Thomas Szasz and R.D. Laing. Each regards "abnormal" conditions as existentially human and hence fundamentally normal. They become psychiatric conditions when looked at psychiatrically. Archetypal psychology, however, makes three further moves beyond anti-psychiatry. First, it examines the normalizing perspective itself in order to show its "abnormalities" and pathologizing propensities. Second, unlike Szasz and Laing, archetypal psychology maintains the real existence of psychopathology as such, as inherent to psychic reality. It neither denies psychopathology nor attempts to find cause for it outside the soul in politics, professional power, or social convention (Foucault). Third, because pathologizing is inherent to psyche, it is also necessary. The necessity of pathologizing derives, on the one hand, from the gods who show patterns of psychopathology and, on the other hand, from the soul, which becomes aware of its destiny in death mainly through the psyche's indefatigable and amazingly inventive capacity to pathologize.

As Freud's paradigm of psychopathology was hysteria (and paranoia) and Jung's was schizophrenia, archetypal psychology has so far spoken mainly about depression (Hillman 1972c, 1975a,c,d, 1979a; Vitale 1973; Berry 1975, 1978b; Guggenbühl-Craig 1979; Miller 1981b; Simmer 1981) and mood disorder (Sardello 1980b). Depression has also provided a focus for *Kulturkritik*, an attack upon social and medical conventions that do not allow the vertical depth of depressions.

For a society that does not allow its individuals "to go down" cannot find its depth and must remain permanently inflated in a manic mood disorder disguised as "growth." Hillman (1975a) links the Western horror of depression with the tradition of the heroic ego and Christian salvation through upward resurrection: "Depression is still the Great Enemy ... Yet through depression we enter depths and in depths find soul. Depression is essential to the tragic sense of life. It moistens the dry soul and dries the wet. It brings refuge, limitation, focus, gravity, weight, and humble powerlessness. It reminds of death. The true revolution (in behalf of soul) begins in the individual who can be true to his or her depression."

12

The Practice of Therapy

Archetypal psychology continues the ritual procedures of classical analysis deriving from Freud and Jung: (1) regular meetings; (2) with individual patients; (3) face-to-face; (4) at the therapist's locus; (5) for a fee. (Groups, couples, and children are generally eschewed; minor attention is paid to diagnostic and typological categories and to psychological testing.) These five procedures, however, are not rigid, and any of them may be modified or abandoned. Classical analysis (Hillman 1975*b*) has been defined as "a course of treatment in an atmosphere of sympathy and confidence of one person by another person for a fee, which treatment may be conceived as educative in various senses or therapeutic in various senses and which proceeds principally through the joint interpretative exploration of habitual behavior and of classes of mental events that have been traditionally called fantasies, feelings, memories, dreams and ideas, and where the exploration follows a coherent set of methods, concepts and beliefs stemming mainly from Freud and from Jung, where focus is preferably upon the unanticipated and affectively charged, and whose goal is the improvement (subjectively and/or objectively determined) of the analysand and the termination of the treatment."

If analysis "terminates," then it is governed by linear time. Casey (1979) exposes this assumption: "...the time of soul is not to be presumed continuous...it is discontinuous, not simply as having breaks or gaps...but as having many avatars, many kinds and modes. The polycentricity of the psyche demands no less than this, namely, a polyform time..." That analyses have been growing longer since the early years with Freud and Jung must be understood as a phenomenon of the soul's temporality: "It is the soul, after all, that is taking all this extra time, and it must be doing so for reasons of its own which have primarily to do with ... taking more world-time so as to encourage the efflorescence of its own imaginal time" (ibid.).

Practice is rooted in Jung's view of the psyche as inherently purposeful: all psychic events whatsoever have *telos*. Archetypal psychology, however, does not enunciate this telos. Purposefulness qualifies psychic events, but it is not to be literalized apart from the images in which it inheres. Thus archetypal psychology refrains from stating goals for therapy (individuation or wholeness) and for its phenomena such as symptoms and dreams (compensations, warnings, prophetic indications). Purpose remains a *perspective* toward events in Jung's original description of the prospective versus the reductive view. Positive formulations of the telos of analysis lead only into teleology and dogmas of goals. Archetypal psychology fosters the sense of purpose as therapeutic in itself because it enhances the patient's interest in psychic phenomena, including the most objectionable symptoms, as intentional. But the therapist does not literalize these intentions, and therefore therapy follows the Freudian mode of restraint and abstention. It moves along a *via negativa*, attempting to deliteralize all formulations of purpose so that the analysis is reduced to sticking with the actual images.

The specific focus and atmosphere of archetypal psychology's way of working and further departures from classical analysis must be culled from many publications for two reasons: there is no program of training (no didactic), and no single work lays out the theory of the practice of therapy. (Publications particularly relevant are: Guggenbühl-Craig 1970, 1971, 1972, 1979; Berry 1978a, 1981; Hillman and Berry 1977; Grinnell 1973; Frey, Bosnak et al. 1978; Giegerich 1977; Hillman 1975a, 1972a, 1964, 1977b and c, 1975c, 1974a; Hartman 1980; Newman 1980; Watkins 1981.)

Departures from classical analysis lie less in the form of therapy than in its focus. Archetypal psychology conceives therapy, as it does psychopathology, as the enactment of fantasy. Rather than prescribe or employ therapy for pathology, it self-examines the fantasy of therapy (so that therapy does not perpetuate the literal pathology which calls therapy forth and is called forth by a literal therapy). Archetypal psychology seeks to remind therapy of its notions of itself (Giegerich 1977), attempting to lift repression from the unconsciousness of therapy itself.

In "The Fiction of Case History," Hillman (1975c) examines the case model used by Freud, and by analysts ever since, as a style of narrative. At once, the problem of cases and the problems told by cases become the subject of an imaginative, literary reflection of which the clinical is only one genre. Genres or categories of the literary imagination – epic, detective, comic, social realist, picaresque – become relevant for understanding the organization of narratives told in therapy. Since "the way we tell our story is the way we form our therapy" (Berry 1974), the entire procedure of therapeutic work must be re-conceived in terms of the poetic basis of mind. An essential work of therapy is to become conscious of the fictions in which the patient is cast and to re-write or ghost-write, collaboratively, the story by re-telling it in a more profound and authentic style. In this re-told version in which imaginative art becomes the model, the personal failures and sufferings of the patient are essential to the story as they are to art.

The *explication du texte* (with which the examination in therapy of images and narrative details can be compared) derives in part from the "personal construct theory" (1955) of George Kelly (b. 1905; d. 1966). Experience is never raw or brute; it is always constructed by images which are revealed in the patient's narrations. The fantasy in which a problem is set tells more about the way the problem is constructed and how it can be transformed (reconstructed) than does any attempt at analyzing the problem in its own terms.

A paper presented by Hillman and Berry at the First International Seminar of Archetypal Psychology (January 1977) declares: "Ours could be called an *image-focused therapy*. Thus the dream as an image or bundle of images is paradigmatic, as if we were placing the entire psychotherapeutic procedure within the context of a dream" (cf. Berry 1974, 1978a, and Hillman 1977b, 1978, 1979a, b, for method and examples of dream work). It is not, however, that dreams as such become the focus of therapy but that all events are regarded from a dream viewpoint, as if they were images, metaphorical expressions. The dream is not in the patient and something he or she does or makes; the patient is in the dream and is doing or being made by its fiction. These same papers on dream work exhibit how an image can be created, that is, how an event can be heard as metaphor through various manipulations: grammatical

reversals, removal of punctuation, restatement and echo, humor, amplification. The aim of working life events as dreams is to bring reflection
to declarative and unreflected discourse, so that words no longer believe
they refer to objective referents; instead, speech becomes imagistic,
self-referent, descriptive of a psychic condition as its very expression
(Berry 1982).

The detailed examination of presentational images – whether from
dreams, from life situations, or the waking imagination of fantasy – has
been a subject for Watkins (1976); Garufi (1977); Humbert (1971); Berry
(1979a,b); Hillman (1977a,c). Here the work is a further refinement of
Jung's technique of "active imagination" (Hull 1971).

Active imagination at times becomes the method of choice in therapy. There is direct perception of and engagement with an imaginary
figure or figures. These figures with whom one converses or performs
actions or which one depicts plastically are not conceived to be merely
internal projections or only parts of the personality. They are given
the respect and dignity due independent beings. They are imagined
seriously, though *not literally*. Rather like Neoplatonic *daimones*, and like
angels in Corbin's sense, their "between" reality is neither physical nor
metaphysical, although just "as real as you – as a psychic entity – are
real" (*CW* 14:753). This development of true imaginative power (the
vera imaginatio of Paracelsus; the *himma* of the heart of Corbin) and the
ability to live one's life in the company of ghosts, familiars, ancestors,
guides – the populace of the metaxy – are also aims of an archetypal
therapy (Hillman 1977c, 1979c).

Recently, image-focused therapy has extended into the sensate world
of perceptual objects and habitual forms – buildings, bureaucratic systems, conventional language, transportation, urban environment, food,
education. This project has no less an ambition than the recuperation of
the *anima mundi* or soul of the world by scrutinizing the face of the world
as aesthetic physiognomy. This move envisages therapy altogether beyond the encounter of two persons in private and takes on the larger task
of re-imagining the public world within which the patient lives (Ogilvy
1977). This notion of therapy attempts to realize the poetic basis of mind
in actuality, as an imaginative, aesthetic response. When the environment
is recognized as imagistic, then each person reacts to it in a more psycho-

logical manner, thereby extending both the notion of the "psychological" to the aesthetic and the notion of therapy from occasional hours in the consulting room to a continual imaginative activity in the home, the street, while eating, or watching television.

Feeling

The liberation of therapy from the exclusivity of the consulting room first requires a re-evaluation of the identity psyche = feeling, that identification of the individual with emotion, which has characterized all schools of psychotherapy ever since Freud's work with conversion hysteria, emotional abreaction, and transference. In brief, therapy has been concerned with personal feeling, and the patient's images have been reduced to his feelings. Hillman (1960, 1971), in two books devoted to emotion and to feeling, began a phenomenological and differentiated analysis of the notions and theories of feeling and emotion as an avenue toward releasing therapy, and psychology itself, from the inevitable narrowing into personalism occasioned by the identification of soul with feeling. The main argument against the personal confessional mode of therapy (Hillman 1979c) – besides its perpetuating the Cartesian division of ensouled subject/lifeless object – is that it fosters the delusion of ownership of emotion, as belonging to the proprium (Allport 1955). The intensified singleness that emotions bring, their narrowing monocentristic effect upon consciousness, gives support to the already monotheistic tendency of the ego to appropriate and identify with its experiences. Emotions reinforce ego psychology. Moreover, when emotion and feeling are conceived as primary, images must play a secondary role. They are considered to be derivative and descriptive of feelings.

Instead, archetypal psychology reverses the relation of feeling and image: feelings are considered to be, as William Blake said, "divine influxes," accompanying, qualifying, and energizing images. They are not merely personal but belong to imaginal reality, the reality of the image, and help make the image felt as a specific value. Feelings elaborate its complexity, and feelings are as complex as the image that contains them. Not images represent feelings, but feelings are inherent to images. Berry (1974) writes: "A dream image is or has the quality of emotion ... They [emotions] adhere or inhere to the image and may not be explicit at all … We cannot entertain any image in dreams, or poetry or painting, without experiencing an emotional quality presented by the image itself." This further implies that any event experienced as an image is at once animated, emotionalized, and placed in the realm of value.

The task of therapy is to return personal feelings (anxiety, desire, confusion, boredom, misery) to the specific images that hold them. Therapy attempts to individualize the face of each emotion: the body of desire, the face of fear, the situation of despair. Feelings are imagined into their details. This move is similar to that of the imagist theory of poetry (Hulme 1924), where any emotion not differentiated by a specific image is inchoate, common, and dumb, remaining both sentimentally personal and yet collectively unindividualized.

13
Eros

S ince its inception, depth psychology has consistently recognized the special role of eros in its work. In fact, psychoanalysis has been as much an eroto-analysis as an analysis of soul, since its basic perspective toward soul has been libidinal. The omnipresence of eros in therapy and in the theory of all depth psychologies receives this recognition under the technical term transference.

Archetypal psychology, analogously to Jung's alchemical psychology of transference, imagines transference against a mythical background – the Eros and Psyche mythologem from Apuleius's *Golden Ass* (Hillman 1972c) – thereby de-historicizing and de-personalizing the phenomenology of love in therapy as well as in any human passion. "By recognizing the primacy of the image, archetypal thought frees both psyche and logos to an Eros that is imaginal" (Bedford 1981). The imaginal, mythical transposition implies that all erotic phenomena whatsoever, including erotic symptoms, seek psychological consciousness and that all psychic phenomena whatsoever, including neurotic and psychotic symptoms, seek erotic embrace. Wherever psyche is the subject of endeavor or the perspective taken toward events, erotic entanglements will necessarily occur because the mythological tandem necessitates their appearance together. While Apuleius's myth details the obstacles in the relation between love and soul, R. Stein (1974) has developed an archetypal approach to the incestuous family hindrances that prevent eros from becoming psychological and psyche from becoming erotic.

The idea of a mythic tandem as basis of transference was first suggested by Freud's Oedipal theory and elaborated by Jung in his anima-animus theory (*CW* 16). Archetypal psychology has gone on to describe a variety of tandems: Senex and Puer (Hillman 1967b, *UE* 3); Venus and Vulcan (M. Stein 1973); Pan and the Nymphs (Hillman

1972*a*); Apollo and Daphne; Apollo and Dionysus; Hermes and Apollo (López-Pedraza 1977); Zeus and Hera (M. Stein 1977); Artemis and Puer (Moore 1979*a*); Echo and Narcissus (Berry 1979*b*); Demeter and Persephone (Berry 1975); Mother and Son (Hillman 1973*b*). Guggenbühl-Craig has discussed the archetypal fantasies operating in the patient-helper relationship (1971) and in the dyad of marriage (1977). These tandems provide occasion for the examination of diverse forms of erotic relationships, their rhetorics and expectations, the particular styles of suffering, and the interlocking mutualities that each tandem imposes. These tandems are imagined also as going on intrapsychically, as patterns of relations between complexes within an individual.

Since love of soul is also love of image, archetypal psychology considers transference, including its strongest sexualized demonstrations, to be a phenomenon of imagination. Nowhere does the impersonality of myth strike a human life more personally. Thus transference is the paradigm for working through the relations of personal and literal with the impersonal and imaginal. Transference is thus nothing less than the eros required by the awakening of psychic reality; and this awakening imposes archetypal roles upon patient and therapist, not the least of which is that of "psychological patient," which means one who suffers or is impassioned by psyche. For this erotic – not medical – reason, archetypal psychology retains the term "patient" instead of client, analysand, trainee, etc. The erotic struggles in any relationship are also psychological struggles with images, and as this *psychomachia* proceeds in an archetypal therapy, there is a transformation of love from a repression and/or obsession with images to a slow love of them, to a recognition that love is itself rooted in images, their continuous creative appearance and their love for that particular human soul in which they manifest.

14

Personality Theory: Personifying

Archetypal psychology's personality theory differs fundamentally from the main views of personality in Western psychology. If pathologizing belongs to the soul and is not to be combated by a strong ego, and if therapy consists in giving support to the counter-ego forces, the personified figures who are ego-alien, then both the theory of psychopathology and that of therapy assume a personality theory that is not ego-centered.

The first axiom of this theory is based on the late development of Jung's complex theory (1946), which holds that every personality is essentially multiple (CW 8:388ff.). Multiple personality is humanity in its natural condition. In other cultures these multiple personalities have names, locations, energies, functions, voices, angel and animal forms, and even theoretical formulations as different kinds of soul. In our culture the multiplicity of personality is regarded either as a psychiatric aberration or, at best, as unintegrated introjections or partial personalities. The psychiatric fear of multiple personality indicates the identification of personality with a partial capacity, the "ego," which is in turn the psychological enactment of a two-thousand-year monotheistic tradition that has elevated unity over multiplicity.

Archetypal psychology extends Jung's personified naming of the components of personality – shadow, anima, animus, trickster, old wise man, great mother, etc. "Personifying or imagining things" (Hillman 1975a) becomes crucial for moving from an abstract, objectified psychology to one that encourages animistic engagement with the world. Personifying further allows the multiplicity of psychic phenomena to be experienced as voices, faces, and names. Psychic phenomena can then be perceived with precision and particularity, rather than generalized in the manner of faculty psychology as feelings, ideas, sensations, and the like.

For archetypal psychology, consciousness is given with the various "partial" personalities. Rather than being imagined as split-off fragments of the "I," they are better reverted to the differentiated models of earlier psychologies where the complexes would have been called souls, daimones, genii, and other mythical-imaginal figures. The consciousness that is postulated *a priori* with these figures or personifications is demonstrated by their interventions in ego control, i.e., the psychopathology of everyday life (Freud), disturbances of attention in the association experiments (Jung), the willfulness and aims of figures in dreams, the obsessive moods and compulsive thoughts that may intrude during any *abaissment du niveau mental* (Janet). Whereas most psychologies attempt to ban these personalities as disintegrative, archetypal psychology favors bringing non-ego figures to further awareness and considers this tension with the non-ego, which relativizes the ego's surety and single perspective to be a chief occupation of soul-making.

Thus, personality is conceived less in terms of stages in life and development, of typologies of character and functioning, of psycho-energetics toward goals (social, individual, etc.) or of faculties (will, affect, reason) and their balance. Rather, personality is imaginatively conceived as a living and peopled drama in which the subject "I" takes part but is neither the sole author, nor director, nor always the main character. Sometimes he or she is not even on the stage. At other times, the other theories of personality just reviewed may play their parts as necessary fictions for the drama.

The healthy or mature or ideal personality will thus show cognizance of its dramatically masked and ambiguous situation. Irony, humor, and compassion will be its hallmarks, since these traits bespeak an awareness of the multiplicity of meanings and fates and the multiplicity of intentions embodied by any subject at any moment. The "healthy personality" is imagined less upon a model of natural, primitive, or ancient man with its nostalgia, or upon social-political man with its mission, or bourgeois rational man with its moralism, but instead against the background of artistic man for whom imagining is a style of living and whose reactions are reflexive, animal, immediate. This model is, of course, not meant literally or singly. It serves to stress certain values of personality to which archetypal psychology gives importance: sophistication, complexity, and impersonal profundity; an animal flow with life disregarding concepts of will, choice, and decision; morality as dedication to crafting the soul (soul-making); sensitivity to traditional continuities; the significance of pathologizing and living at the "borders"; aesthetic responsiveness.

15

Biographical

As shown above, archetypal psychology is not a theoretical system emanating from the thought of one person for whom it is named, then identifying with a small group, becoming a school, and moving into the world in the manner of Freudian or Jungian psychologies; nor does it emerge from a particular clinic, laboratory, or city giving it its name. Rather, archetypal psychology presents the polytheistic structure of a postmodern consciousness. It is a style of thinking, a fashion of mind, a revisionist engagement on many fronts: therapy, education, literary criticism, medicine, philosophy, and the material world. It assembles and lends its terms and viewpoints to a variety of intellectual concerns in contemporary thought. Eros and a common concern for soul, image, and pathology draw individuals from diverse geographical and intellectual areas into rapport with each other for the revisioning of their ideas and their worlds.

Inasmuch as the sources are in C.G. Jung and Henry Corbin, the biographical origins can be traced to the Eranos Conferences at Ascona, Switzerland (Rudolf Ritsema), where Jung and Corbin were perennially major speakers. Gilbert Durand and James Hillman entered that circle in the 1960s; David L. Miller in the 1970s; Alfred Ziegler and Wolfgang Giegerich in the 1980s. The Platonist inspiration at Eranos, its concern for spirit in a time of crisis and decay, the mutuality of engagement that transcends academic specialization, and the educative effect of eros on soul were together formative in the directions that archetypal psychology was subsequently to take.

A second biographical strand can be discerned in a period (April 1969) at the Warburg Institute in London and the confrontation by Rafael López-Pedraza, Hillman, and Patricia Berry with the tradition of classical (pagan, polytheistic) images in the Western psyche. Here they found witness to a ground for psychology in the cultural imagination, especially of the Mediterranean, which would allow psychology to return from its distractions by natural science and Eastern spirituality. Third was the refounding, in 1970, in Zurich of the Jungian journal *Spring* as an organ of archetypal thought and the launching of other publications, as well as seminars on psychological readings of Renaissance images.

Fourth, subsequent developments took place in the Western Hemisphere. In February 1972, the invitation to give the distinguished Dwight Harrington Terry Lectures at Yale University enabled Hillman (1975*a*) to present the first comprehensive formulation of archetypal psychology. This was followed by the appointment of Hillman and Berry as visiting lecturers in the Yale psychology faculty, where their association with the Yale philosopher Edward S. Casey turned their work toward mutual explorations of the philosophy of imagination and phenomenology. During the mid-seventies, graduate degree programs were being established at Sonoma State, California (Gordon Tappan), and the University of Dallas (Robert Sardello). In 1976, Hillman and Berry joined the faculty of the Department of Religions at Syracuse University, New York, and in collaboration with Miller worked further into the problems of monotheistic and polytheistic thinking. In January 1977, partly sponsored by a grant from the Rockefeller Brothers Foundation, archetypal psychology held its first International Seminar at the University of Dallas, gathering together some twenty of the individuals mentioned in this article. Other conferences and seminars were held at the University of Notre Dame, Indiana (Thomas Kapacinskas); Duquesne University, Pennsylvania; and the University of New Mexico (Howard McConeghey). In January 1978, the University of Dallas appointed Hillman a professor of psychology and Berry a visiting professor.

Meanwhile, López-Pedraza had been appointed a lecturer in mythology and psychology in the Faculty of Letters at the University of Caracas. With the opening (in 1981) of the Dallas Institute of Humanities and Culture (whose Fellows include Sardello, Thomas Moore, Joanne Stroud, Gail Thomas, and Hillman), archetypal psychology turned toward the "soul in the world" (*anima mundi*) of the city. "City" becomes the patient, the place of pathologizing, and the locus where the soul's imagination is actualized on earth, requiring an archetypally psychological perspective for examining its ills.

No nation in Europe has responded more attentively to this revisionist thought than Italy. A number of engaged intellectuals and therapists in Rome, Florence, Pisa, and Milan have succeeded in translating (Aldo Giuliani) works of archetypal psychology in the *Rivista di psicologia analitica*, in books (Adelphi, Communitá), and in publications of the *Enciclopedia Italiana*, and have presented its thought in teaching, editing, and translating (Francesco Donfrancesco, Bianca Garufi). In France, a similar initiative, joining with the groups affiliated with Corbin and Durand, was pioneered by Editions Imago, by Michel Cazenave and by Monique Salzmann.

Two European events – a world conference in Cordoba on "Science and Consciousness" (Cazenave 1980), reflecting the thought of Jung and Corbin and the Eranos circle (Miller, Toshihiko Izutsu, Durand, Kathleen Raine, Hillman) in relation with contemporary physical sciences, and an address by Hillman (1982) on archetypal psychology as a Renaissance psychology in Florence (Donfrancesco) – have presented what is reviewed in this essay in the wide current of contemporary Western ideas.

Postscript

The fifteen short chapters above could each be carried further in light of work produced since 1981, but such extensions would stretch this brief account beyond its original purpose: an article for the *Enciclopedia del Novecento*. The following new chapters document later directions in the field. The new chapters serve also to pick up themes somewhat neglected in 1981, largely because they were hardly emerging then, whereas now they are major components of archetypal psychology's basis and focus.

A word about the term "archetypal psychology": When first introduced (Hillman 1970*b*), it was considered a replacement for "analytical" psychology as Jung's opus had come to be called. Because "archetypal" was both broader and descriptively more faithful to Jung's main concern – the deepest nature of the psyche's realities – the term better presented his work. In fact, "archetypal" can incorporate "analytical" as one of the many methods for encountering those psychic realities.

As time has gone on, "archetypal" has had to define itself again. This time in contrast with the more substantive, essentialist use of the word archetype, or what philosophy calls reification and hypostatization – archetypes as things. The substantive approach tends to tie archetypes with entities of biology, or physics, or metaphysics in a remote Platonic pleroma, and to make statements about them in a quasi-theological manner. "An Inquiry into Image" (*Spring: An Annual of Archetypal Psychology and Jungian Thought* [1977]), by employing Occam's famous logical razor, questioned the possibility of saying anything at all about entities that are, according to Jung, unknowable in themselves. We can only infer "archetypal" from phenomenal appearances, that is, as archetypal images (cf. Chapter 3 above).

The humbling of the term from noun to adjectival and adverbial qualifier, from thing to quality, leads to the conclusion that "archetypal" is a value term. It qualifies an event with such values as universality, emotionality, timelessness, fecundity, aesthetic force, irreducibility, and possibly also animation.

"Archetypal psychology" means a psychology not based on things called archetypes as much as a revaluation of psychology itself as an archetypal activity that restores to the phenomena it addresses the value and intensified significance that Alfred North Whitehead (1938) called "importance."

16

Animals

Besides C.G. Jung and Henry Corbin (cf. Chapter 1), a third "father" deserves honoring: Adolf Portmann, the eminent Swiss zoologist whose originality, judgment, and inspiration led the Eranos conferences from the early 1960s until his death in the late 1970s. Portmann's approach to biology opened the way to an aesthetic reading of life's phenomena. Form, color, pattern, movement, interrelatedness reveal the self-display of animals as living images (Bleakley 2000; Hillman and McLean 1997 and *UE* 9). The animal's inwardness (*Innerlichkeit*) is afforded by its self-display (*Selbstdarstellung*), that is, it presents itself as an image affording (Gibson 1950) intelligibility to its surround. Archetypal psychology relies on both Portmann and Gibson for understanding perceived presence as available inwardness. Reading the world requires an "animal eye" of aesthetic perception and an "animal body" of aesthetic responses. Portmann's biology of living forms adds an animal dimension to the Neoplatonic idea of inherent intelligibility of all things, sometimes elaborated as the Doctrine of Signatures (visible markings indicate invisible potencies).

The primary qualifier of consciousness becomes participatory awareness – already indicated by the prefix *con* (with). Participation may include all kinds of image presences such as dreams, projects, memories, feelings, and is not restricted to the palpable world. Reflection, however, the major characteristic of consciousness in Jung's psychology (*CW* 8: 241–43; 11: 235n) takes a more secondary place. Unconsciousness, rather than defined as unreflected, means isolate, anaesthetized, unresponsive to affording images.

The immediacy of the world afforded by the image to the animal eye and animal body bears upon other ideas important to archetypal psychology, e.g. Vico's *certum*, Santayana's "animal faith," Grinnell's (1970) "psychological faith," and Hillman's (1990) "mythical certitude."

There is also a resemblance here with Levinas's (1969) immediacy of the face that evokes a compelling ethical response. Archetypal psychology embeds human existence within an animalized, animated world, not because the human has fallen into it owing to sin or is evolving out of it toward a higher condition, but because the psyche, as Aristotle said, is the forming idea of a living body.

17

Anima Mundi

At the Eranos meeting of 1977, the idea was first broached of a "depth psychology of extraversion" (Hillman 1980). This move both critically questioned subjective introversion as the defining criterion of depth of soul and inclusively widened psychological depth to mean interiority of the "outer" world. This promiscuity of depth has its antecedent in a statement attributed to the early Greek philosopher Thales: "All things are full of gods."

Soul-in-the-world-of-things also refers back to the Platonic cosmic principle of *anima mundi*. By reading the term *mundi* not only to mean *of* the world, or world soul as a Romantic over-soul, but more immanently as *in* the world, archetypal psychology brings the Platonic vision down to earth. This reading (or misreading) of *mundi* implies that both natural world and made world can be subject to psychological analysis. Confining analysis to human subjectivity is a restriction of method that distorts psychological realities. A lecture held at the Palazzo Vecchio in Florence in 1981 (Hillman 1996) under the auspices of Donfrancesco (and appropriately announced by trumpets) heralded this return to the world.

From there it was an easy step for archetypal psychology to move in a variety of directions:

> (*a*) urbanism and architecture in conjunction with the Dallas Institute of Humanities and Culture, engendering discussion in other cities – Pittsburgh, Buffalo, Fort Worth, Trento, Chiavari, Siracusa;
>
> (*b*) conferences and seminars under the auspices of the Esalen Institute, Big Sur, California; the Omega Institute, Rhinebeck, New York; the Pacifica Graduate Institute, Carpinteria, California;

and the Schumacher College, Dartington, England; each of which focused on the psyche of environment;

(c) men's retreats that activated ritual animation of environment and aesthetic sensitivity (Michael Meade, Robert Bly, Enrique Pardo, Coleman Barks, Gary Snyder, Malidoma Somé);

(d) a long-term study group initiated by Charles Halpern at the Nathan Cummings Foundation, New York, that brought together artists, psychologists, philosophers, activists, lawyers, teachers, etc.;

(e) objects and natural phenomena as agents, affecting co-actors in theatrical dramas (Enrique Pardo, Nor Hall), or leaving traces of their movement (animation) in artworks (Sandy Gellis).

As work in these directions progressed, it became evident that the repressed unconscious was no longer childhood and family matters, personal relationships and instinctual urges, nor even "self"-realization, but beauty and justice. Ugliness and injustice have become the most basic miseries afflicting the collective psyche of humans and world alike.

Beauty has been addressed by several psychologists (Thomas Moore, Ronald Schenk, Noel Cobb, David McLagan, Francesco Donfrancesco) and presented in dramatic/visual forms (Enrique Pardo, Mark Kidel, Nor Hall, Rafael López-Pedraza, Margot McLean). Taking a cue from Plotinus who said the soul is always Aphrodite, beauty is necessarily a dominant mode of exploring the anima mundi. Robert Lifton's idea of "psychic numbing" that characterizes citizens since Hiroshima can be rephrased as anesthesia, the loss of the aesthetic response, a response which is also ethical (Levinas 1969) and is therefore also a political action (Hillman 1999). Beauty and justice interlinked have been the aim of soul work ever since Socrates (Hillman 2001) and were declared the fundamental principles of an ecological psychotherapy by Hillman on the occasion of his receiving the medal of the President of the Italian Republic in 2000.

The extension into the world, which breaks therapeutic psychology out of clinical literalism with its diagnostic pretensions and case management methods, has become a common trust of the core faculty at the Pacifica Graduate Institute. David Miller, Christine Downing, Dennis Slattery, Ginette Paris, Mary Watkins, Robert Romanyshyn have each been rethinking the depth psychology of extraversion in relation with their individual callings. For instance, Miller has brought new reflection to the archetypal images at work in teaching, Paris to the myths patterning usual human existence, while Watkins has initiated psychological field work with an idea of the "unconscious" so that the term refers to the neglected, marginalized and oppressed in society. Dreams, too, cannot be located exclusively within the human psyche, but speak to and from the world itself (Stephen Aizenstaat, Robert Bosnak).

18

Place

The topic of Chapter 9, "Cultural Locus: North and South," is proving fruitful. Ideas emerging from Latin America evidenced in the Bibliography (Part Two) show a fertility of fantasy that is at once aesthetic and social; i.e., a psychology rooted within ex-colonial political realities and precolonial indigenous cultures. In contrast, the move "south" in Europe focuses more on the return to the classical and pagan Mediterranean, Dionysus, and the arrival of Sicily on the map of Italian archetypal psychology. "South" in the United States symbolizes with down, below, fertile and dark, and so it is explored in terms of the psyche of the inner city (Michael Meade, Aaron Kipnis); prisons (Susan Still, Leslie Neale, Bob Roberts); black (Michael Vannoy Adams, Stanton Marlan); and writers in the Haiti issue, *Spring* 61 (1998).

The power of place (Casey 1993, 1997) as a determining fantasy in thought and action makes place an axiomatic foundation in archetypal psychology, buttressing further its arguments against universalism, metaphysical abstractions, mathematical reductions, and the exaggerations of the scientific *Weltbild* in search of a unified field theory. Psychological ecumenism, e.g., Freudian-Jungian harmonies, would be another example of the neglect of place since Jungian (if not Freudian) psychology has differentiated into a multiplicity of geographical varieties.

Emphasis upon the eachness (William James) of place and the close attention to its specifics, e.g., the scene of a dream event, the place of a memory, further favor the soul's idiosyncratic constellations protecting them from spiritual formulae for ameliorating the human condition (Cf. Chapter 6).

Place itself is an abstraction unless returned to the ancient idea of a *genius loci*, a specific local daimon that was foundational to places in the pagan world for the siting of temples (Scully 1962), dreaming and healing centers like Epidauros, initiatory cults like Eleusis, and prophesy like Dodona and Delphi. From the beginning of Western therapeutics (Hippocrates' Airs, Waters, Places) a sense of place informs psychological practice. A therapist situates a patient not merely in a universal diagnostic category, but more accurately within a set of mores, accents, cooking and clothing that shape a diagnosis and give it a "local habitatation and a name."

Cultural location implies more than location as such. The move south can be imagined as going downward (for the Northern mind) into "body" and into lower economic strata mentioned in Chapter 17, and also into the receptive, fecund, yin-like characteristics of the soul. Another fruitful opening southward is linguistic and rhetorical – the move from concept to image including phonetic image (Paul Kugler) and the importance of a musical hearing (Thomas Moore) for metaphorical recognition. Poetry plays an unusually significant role in the background of archetypal psychology for reasons explained in Chapter 2.

The fact that archetypal psychology has shown vigor in three regions where language is still strongly imagistic and metaphorical – Italian, Portuguese, Japanese – can also be understood as the move southward.

The idea of place has given us the word "pagan." Paganus referred to native peoples mainly in the countryside in distinction to *alieni* – members of foreign militia, occupiers, administrators who came from elsewhere. "Pagan" as the term developed in Christian vocabulary means simply the religious practices of a localized homeland. The definition of pagan as the people of a place and defenders of this-place-here against the alienation brought by universalist science and religion necessitates archetypal psychology's turn toward ecological and urban concerns. The place consciousness and place priority of environmentalism is paganism up-to-date: tree-huggers recapitulating the tree-worshipers of sacred groves. Environmentalism as paganism in contemporary dress has not escaped the notice of, and condemnation by, Christian public officials (*alieni*) in their resistance to fervent environmental protection. Though the pagan way of life assumes the animation of the daily environment – that the world addresses you, speaks to you, and both tempts and guides you – Christianity, too, recognizes the *genius loci* in its sacred sites for pilgrimage, martyrs' graves, healing miracles, saintly visions, and vaults of holy bones.

A caution is necessary: place is not to be sought only in literal geographies. Already Hillman's 1972 Terry Lectures (1975a) spoke of the return to Greece as an imaginal place. Corbin's geographical descriptions recounted from Islamic texts are "nowhere" places, utopic, yet each with its coloration and climate, gardens and mountains. St. Augustine's interiority of soul is placed within a cavernous region, as are the halls of Hades.

"Whereness" is essential to archetypal psychology for grounding the poetic palpability of phenomena encountered.

These locations, even when pinpointed to a hometown street corner with names and numbers, are also always a geography of imagination writhing with memories, creatures, villains, and half-buried cultural shards awaiting discovery.

19

Practice

Institutions differ in regard to the contents required for training depth psychologists. Institutions, however, all follow the apprentice system in refining the skills of the novice candidate. Practice, like hard work, is learned by handling the case, and the craft is handed down from seniors to juniors who submit to supervision. The superior sort of vision of the supervisor enables both parties to hear into the background of the case exposed. Following Freud, this background is called "the unconscious." Since the most unconscious patterns requiring superior insight are archetypal, following Jung, myths provide the most functional representation of what plays out in the dilemmas of practice. The supervisor needs to have in mind a thesaurus of mythemes in order to do his/her work competently (Adams 2001, 2002). Specific myths and mythical figures in relation to human troubles and potentials have been explored by Deldon McNeely (Hermes), Noel Cobb (Orpheus), Sandra Edelman (Athene), Sherry Salmon (Furies), and in collections edited by Joanne Stroud (the Olympians) and Gail Thomas (the Muses).

Knowledge of myth and structures of the imaginal (Gilbert Durand) require more than the study of mythology as such. Political, social, and religious history repeat archetypal patterns; fiction, film, folktale, drama, and the plastic arts too, are structured by myths (Paris 1986, 1990). Vladimir Propp, Stith Thompson, Georges Polti, Eleazar Meletinsky (1976), Hedwig von Beit, and Marie-Louise von Franz have catalogued many of the basic themes. The research tools developed by Ginette Paris and by William Doty for accessing mythical images and motifs open the way for therapy of soul to draw on the images of culture.

If the psyche's disorders portray the autonomy of the imagination, then appreciating them with amplification, as Jung did in his early masterwork *Symbols of Transformation* (CW5), becomes the hallmark of practice. Yet, it is here that Jungian psychology, as it seeks to become more ecumenical, academic, institutional, and to train disciples, parts ways most sharply with an archetypal approach to practice. The index to the main compendium on training (Kugler 1995) has two entries for myths, sixteen for management, and a multitude for transference. Whereas Corbett, Ulanov, Speicher, and Henderson in that volume recognize that transference is played out in a variety of configurations (Jung elaborated only one, e.g., the alchemical mode), the fundamental idea of transference is left untouched, i.e., transference is a myth-like happening in a ritual enclosure. It conjures forces that are not personal, not rational, and perhaps not altogether human. Mythical understanding thus becomes crucial since myths, according to Vico, set the unruly imagination on course; that is, they are therapeutic *per se*. And why? Again Vico, because they are *universali fantastici;* a myth is *vera narratio*. It speaks truth.

Though mythology is necessary for practice, the basic reason for this study is the transformation of insight. One learns to see the fictional nature of clinical fact. The practitioner moves from recognizing myths in life to the recognition of life as myth. An archetypal practice may be a work with persons, between persons, within persons, yet it seeks to "dehumanize" (1975a) the literalism of the personal. Therefore this practice feels like a work in a fiction, a work with story, with images, figures, metaphors, rhythms, moods, a work akin to the practice of an art in alchemical seclusion and packed with a peculiar kind of love.

A mythical sense of life leads the practitioner to see through the idea of practice itself, less as an empirical science or a humanistic treatment, education, or relationship, and more as an inventive inquiry into the twisted paths that imagination takes in a human life which the subject feels, and clinical psychology diagnoses, to be pathology.

The inherent relation of mythology and pathology was established for practice at its beginnings by both Freud and Jung. The 1974 Eranos lecture (1974a) introduced the *"infirmitas* of the gods," or pathology of the gods themselves. This takes further Jung's statement that "the gods have become diseases" – because gods are limited and imperfect, each showing its own style of pathology to which it gives an archetypal value.

However, the closeness of mythology and pathology can endanger archetypal psychology with clinical literalism: mythology as nosology; gods and goddesses as labels for disorders; Robert Graves, Walter Otto, Karl Kerényi, et al. replacing the DSM.

If we remember that psyche is a way of seeing and not a thing seen, then myths provide a way of insighting the soul's *pathos* and are as well a way of speaking (*logos*) to it and about it. But myths are not disorders. Psychopathology is irreducible and necessary soul stuff that invites a hermeneutical imagination of many sorts: psychiatric diagnostics, bio-chemical physiology, the fiction of case history and early childhood, karma, alchemy. Myths are but one way of imagining the case. Their one great advantage lies in that they are myths, not empirical facts, not beliefs, and therefore should be able to protect the practitioner from clinical literalism – and also from clinical charlatanism, which magically transforms unreals into the causal realities of disease entities.

An archetypal practice is obliged to extend beyond the clinical in the usual sense of a practice with persons. The world too has its subjectivity and asks to be regarded with a therapeutic eye, else the soul is split away from its larger part (Sendivogius, Paracelsus) beyond the human. Then the burden of the soul's sufferings all falls on to the human and the soul feels trapped in traditional notions of sin: "It's all my fault."

This overload lays the ground for the person's depressive alienation from the world soul and for the motivation to find redemption at any cost. The restriction of "clinical" to the interior subjectivity of humans is a self-serving idea of practical value for the clinician, increasing the self-centered misery in the patient and promoting the grandeur of the clinician to an archetypal significance of savior (Guggenbühl-Craig 1971). Practice as secular *soteriology* (a way of salvation) therefore ne-cessitates emphasis upon countertransference analysis as deconstructive countermeasure to the archetypal empowerment of the clinician.

The extension of therapy from person to world also means the world of ideas, since ideas – such as the idea of "clinical" itself – are determining factors in a patient's distress. "Ideas you have and don't know you have, have you," is an oft-repeated slogan justifying the archetypal analysis of ideas, deepened by David L. Miller in his examination of image-ideas (e.g., shepherd, mirror) for their effects in practice.

Finally, a psychoanalysis of the phenomenal world is based less on phenomenological method or on systems theory of interdependence than on the poetics of Gaston Bachelard. There is an elemental reverie, a mythical imagining going on in the world's stuff much as the soul of the human is always dreaming its myth along. Things transcend themselves in their affordances (Gibson), in their imaginings, which poets from Wordsworth and Coleridge through Borges, Williams, Barthes, Ponge, Oliver, Blakeslee, and Bly (in his own work and his translations) make very clear. Things offer themselves as animals do to one another in their display. Substances themselves project upon each other according to the alchemical definition of projection. Not the human subject but the images invent the ideas we "have." They come in (*invenire*)... .

While phenomenological method teaches how to receive things without prejudgment, letting them speak in their own way (Sardello, Watkins, Romanyshyn, Casey), Corbin's extrapolations from Islamic texts (Cheetham 2003) teach that things as they are always seek to be in tune with another dimension, that music played on Stevens's "blue guitar." Things are never, can never be just as they are by definition, can never be encompassed. Thus the soul, healed and whole as it possibly, ideally may be, still lacks that which is beyond, and which remains out of reach, infinite. That the soul longs, its *pathos* partly an expression of its *pothos*, is the ground of both its imperfection, felt as restlessness and failure, and the creative poiesis in humans and all of nature to produce endless novelty, endless variation in the makings of itself. The soul is always wanting (Hillman 1977c), and this is the reason for the necessity of unfulfillment and why a psychoanalysis of anything to do with soul is, as Freud said, interminable.

Abbreviations

CW = *Collected Works of C.G. Jung,* trans. R.F.C. Hull, 20 vols. (Princeton, N.J.: Princeton University Press, 1953–79), cited by paragraph number unless indicated otherwise.

UE = *The Uniform Edition of the Writings of James Hillman,* 10 vols. (Putnam, Conn.: Spring Publications, 2004–).

References

Adams, Michael Vannoy (2001). *The Mythological Unconscious* (Putnam, Conn.: Spring Publications, 2010).
_____ (2002). "Mythological Knowledge: Just How Important Is It in Jungian (and Freudian) Analysis?" *Harvest: Journal for Jungian Studies* 48, no. 1 (2002).
Allport, Gordon W. (1955). *Becoming: Basic Considerations for a Psychology of Personality* (New Haven: Yale University Press, 1977).
Armstrong, A.H. (1981). "Some Advantages of Polytheism," *Dionysius* 5 (1981).
Armstrong, Robert P. (1971). *The Affecting Presence* (Urbana: University of Illinois Press, 1971).
Avens, Roberts (1980). *Imagination Is Reality: Western Nirvana in Jung, Hillman, Barfield and Cassirer* (Putnam, Conn.: Spring Publications, 2003).
_____ (1982a). "Heidegger and Archetypal Psychology," *International Philosophical Quarterly* 22 (1982).
_____ (1982b). *Imaginal Body: Para-Jungian Reflections on Soul, Imagination and Death* (Washington, D.C.: University Press of America, 1982).
Bachelard, Gaston (1943). *Air and Dreams: An Essay on the Imagination of Movement,* trans. Edith R. and C. Frederick Farrell (Dallas: Dallas Institute Publications, 2002).
Bedford, Gary S. (1981). "Notes on Mythological Psychology," *Journal of the American Academy of Religion* 49 (1981).
Berry, Patricia (1973). "On Reduction," *Spring: An Annual of Archetypal Psychology and Jungian Thought* (1973).
_____ (1974). "An Approach to the Dream," *Spring: An Annual of Archetypal Psychology and Jungian Thought* (1974).
_____ (1975). "The Rape of Demeter/Persephone and Neurosis," *Spring: An Annual of Archetypal Psychology and Jungian Thought* (1975).

_____ (1978a). "Defense and Telos in Dreams," *Spring: An Annual of Archetypal Psychology and Jungian Thought* (1978).

_____ (1978b). *What's the Matter with Mother?* Pamphlet (London: Guild of Pastoral Psychology, 1978).

_____ (1979a). "Virginities of Image." Paper: Dragonflies Conference on Virginity in Psyche, Myth, and Community, University of Dallas, 1979.

_____ (1979b). "Echo's Passion." Paper: Dragonflies Conference on Beauty in Psyche, Myth, and Community, University of Dallas, 1979.

_____ (1981). "The training of shadow and the shadow of training," *Journal of Analytical Psychology* 26 (1981).

_____ (1982). "Hamlet's Poisoned Ear," *Spring: An Annual of Archetypal Psychology and Jungian Thought* (1982).

[The papers of Patricia Berry have subsequently been collected in one volume: *Echo's Subtle Body: Contributions to an Archetypal Psychology* (Putnam, Conn.: Spring Publications, 2008).]

Bleakley, Alan (2000). *The Animalizing Imagination: Totemism, Textuality and Ecocriticism* (New York: St. Martin's Press, 2000).

Boer, Charles, trans. (1980). *Marsilio Ficino: The Book of Life* (Irving, Texas: Spring Publications, 1980).

_____ and Kugler, Peter (1977). "Archetypal Psychology Is Mythical Realism," *Spring: An Annual of Archetypal Psychology and Jungian Thought* (1977).

Bregman, Lucy (1980). "Religious Imagination: Polytheistic Psychology Confronts Calvin," *Soundings* 63 (1980).

Casey, Edward S. (1974). "Toward an Archetypal Imagination," *Spring: An Annual of Archetypal Psychology and Jungian Thought* (1974).

_____ (1976). *Imagining: A Phenomenological Study* (Bloomington: Indiana University Press, 2000).

_____ (1979). "Time in the Soul," *Spring: An Annual of Archetypal Psychology and Jungian Thought* (1979).

_____ (1982). "Getting Placed: Soul in Space," *Spring: An Annual of Archetypal Psychology and Jungian Thought* (1982).

_____ (1993). *Getting Back into Place: Toward a Renewed Understanding of the Place-World* (Bloomington: Indiana University Press, 2009).

_____ (1997). *The Fate of Place: A Philosophical History* (Berkeley: University of California Press, 1998).

Cazenave, Michel (1980). *Two Views of the Universe,* trans. A. Hall and E. Callander (Oxford: Pergamon Press, 1984).

Cheetham, Tom (2003). *The World Turned Inside Out: Henry Corbin and Islamic Mysticism* (Woodstock, Conn.: Spring Journal Books, 2003).

Christou, Evangelos (1963). *The Logos of the Soul,* with a preface by James Hillman (Putnam, Conn.: Spring Publications, 2007).

Cook, Daniel J. (1973). *Language in the Philosophy of Hegel* (The Hague: Mouton, 1973).

Corbin, Henry (1958). *Alone with the Alone: Creative Imagination in the Sufism of Ibn 'Arabî*, trans. R. Manheim (Princeton, N.J.: Princeton University Press, 1998).

_____ (1971–73). *En Islam iranien: Aspects spirituels et philosophique*, 4 vols. (Paris: Gallimard, 1991).

_____ (1977). *Spiritual Body and Celestial Earth: From Mazdean Iran to Shi'ite Iran*, trans. N. Pearson (Princeton, N.J.: Princeton University Press, 1989).

_____ (1979). *Avicenna and the Visionary Recital*, trans. W.R. Trask (Princeton, N.J.: Princeton University Press, 1990).

Cowan, Lyn (1979). "On Masochism," *Spring: An Annual of Archetypal Psychology and Jungian Thought* (1979).

Durand, Gilbert (1960). *Les Structures anthropologiques de l'imaginaire* (Paris: Dunod, 1993).

_____ (1975). *Science de l'homme et tradition* (Paris: Albin Michel, 1996).

_____ (1979). *Figures mythiques et visages de l'oeuvre* (Paris: Berg International, 1979).

Frey-Wehrlin, Caspar Toni, Robert Bosnak, et al. (1978). "The Treatment of Chronic Psychosis," *Journal of Analytical Psychology* 23 (1978).

Garufi, Bianca (1977). "Reflections on the 'rêve éveillé dirigé' method," *Journal of Analytical Psychology* 22 (1977).

Gibson, James Jerome (1950). *The Perception of the Visual World* (Boston: Houghton Mifflin, 1950).

Giegerich, Wolfgang (1977). "On the Neurosis of Psychology," *Spring: An Annual of Archetypal Psychology and Jungian Thought* (1977).

_____ (1982). "Buße für Philemon: Vertiefung in das verdorbene Gast-Spiel der Götter," *Eranos Yearbook* 51 (1982).

Goldenberg, Naomi (1975). "Archetypal Theory after Jung," *Spring: An Annual of Archetypal Psychology and Jungian Thought* (1975).

_____ (1979). *Changing of the Gods: Feminism and the End of Traditional Religion* (Boston: Beacon, 1979).

Grinnell, Robert (1970). "Reflections on the Archetype of Consciousness: Personality and Psychological Faith," *Spring: An Annual of Archetypal Psychology and Jungian Thought* (1970).

_____ (1973). *Alchemy in a Modern Woman: A Study in the Contrasexual Archetype* (Woodstock, Conn.: Spring Publications, 1973).

Guggenbühl-Craig, Adolf (1970). "Must Analysis Fail through Its Destructive Aspect?" *Spring: An Annual of Archetypal Psychology and Jungian Thought* (1970).

_____ (1971). *Power in the Helping Professions*, trans. M. Gubitz (Putnam: Conn.: Spring Publications, 2009).

_____ (1972). "Analytical Rigidity and Ritual," *Spring: An Annual of Archetypal Psychology and Jungian Thought* (1972).

_____ (1977). *Marriage Is Dead – Long Live Marriage!* trans. M. Stein (Putnam, Conn.: Spring Publications, 2008).

_____ (1979). "The Archetype of the Invalid and the Limits of Healing," *Spring: An Annual of Archetypal Psychology and Jungian Thought* (1979).

Hartman, Gary V. (1980). "Psychotherapy: An Attempt at Definition," *Spring: An Annual of Archetypal Psychology and Jungian Thought* (1980).

Hawkins, Ernest (1979). "On Migraine: From Dionysos to Freud," *Dragonflies: Studies in Imaginal Psychology* 1 (1979).

Hillman, James (1960). *Emotion: A Comprehensive Phenomenology of Theories and their Meanings for Therapy* (London: Routledge & Kegan Paul, 1960).

_____ (1964). *Suicide and the Soul* (Putnam, Conn.: Spring Publications, 2004).

_____ (1967a). *Insearch: Psychology and Religion* (Putnam, Conn.: Spring Publications, 2004).

_____ (1967b). "Senex and Puer," in *UE* 3: *Senex & Puer.*

_____ (1970a). "On Senex Consciousness," in *UE* 3: *Senex & Puer.*

_____ (1970b). "Why 'Archetypal' Psychology?" *Spring: An Annual of Archetypal Psychology and Jungian Thought* (1970).

_____ (1971). "The Feeling Function," in *Lectures on Jung's Typology,* with M.-L. von Franz (Putnam, Conn.: Spring Publications, 2010).

_____ (1972a). "An Essay on Pan," in *Pan and the Nightmare,* with W.H. Roscher (Putnam, Conn.: Spring Publications, 2007).

_____ (1972b). "Failure and Analysis," *Journal of Analytical Psychology* 17 (1972).

_____ (1972c). *The Myth of Analysis: Three Essays in Archetypal Psychology* (Evanston, Ill.: Northwestern University Press, 1998).

_____ (1973a). "Plotino, Ficino e Vico precursori della psicologia degli archetipi," *Rivista di Psicologia Analitica* 4 (1973).

_____ (1973b). "The Great Mother, Her Son, Her Hero, and the Puer," in *UE* 3: *Senex & Puer.*

_____ (1973c). "Anima," *Spring: An Annual of Archetypal Psychology and Jungian Thought* (1973).

_____ (1974a). "On the Necessity of Abnormal Psychology," *Eranos Yearbook* 43 (1974). Revised as "Athene, Ananke, and Abnormal Psychology," in *UE* 6: *Mythic Figures.*

_____ (1974b). "Anima II," *Spring: An Annual of Archetypal Psychology and Jungian Thought* (1974).

_____ (1975a). *Re-Visioning Psychology* (New York: Harper & Row, 1975).

_____ (1975b). *Loose Ends: Primary Papers in Archetypal Psychology* (Zurich: Spring Publications, 1975).

_____ (1975c). "The Fiction of Case History," in *Religion as Story,* ed. J.B. Wiggins (New York: Harper & Row, 1975).

_____ (1975d). "Negative Senex and a Renaissance Solution," in *UE* 3: *Senex & Puer.*

_____ (1976). "Peaks and Vales: The Soul/Spirit Distinction as Basis for the Differences between Psychotherapy and Spiritual Discipline," in *UE* 3: *Senex & Puer.*

_____ (1977*a*). "The Pandaemonium of Images: C.G. Jung's Contribution to Know Thyself," *New Lugano Review* 3 (1977).

_____ (1977*b*). "An Inquiry into Image," *Spring: An Annual of Archetypal Psychology and Jungian Thought* (1977).

_____ (1977*c*). "Psychotherapy's Inferiority Complex," *Eranos Yearbook* 46 (1977).

_____ (1978). "Further Notes on Images," *Spring: An Annual of Archetypal Psychology and Jungian Thought* (1978).

_____ (1979*a*). *The Dream and the Underworld* (New York: Harper & Row, 1979).

_____ (1979*b*). "Image-Sense," *Spring: An Annual of Archetypal Psychology and Jungian Thought* (1979).

_____ (1979*c*). "The Thought of the Heart," *Eranos Yearbook* 48 (1979).

_____ (1980). "Egalitarian Typologies versus the Perception of the Unique," *Eranos Yearbook* 45 (1980).

_____ (1981*a*). "Silver and the White Earth," in *UE* 5: *Alchemical Psychology.*

_____ (1981*b*). "Alchemical Blue and the Unio Mentalis," in *UE* 5: *Alchemical Psychology.*

_____ (1982). "Anima mundi: The Return of the Soul to the World," *Spring: An Annual of Archetypal Psychology and Jungian Thought* (1982).

_____ (1990). "On Mythical Certitude," *Sphinx: A Journal for Archetypal Psychology and the Arts* 3 (1990).

_____ (1996). *The Thought of the Heart and the Soul of the World* (Putnam, Conn.: Spring Publications, 2007).

_____ and Margot McLean (1997). *Dream Animals* (San Francisco: Chronicle, 1997). Reprinted in *UE* 9: *Animal Presences.*

_____ (1999). "La risposta estetica come azione politica" (Aesthetic Response as Political Action), in *Politica della bellezza*, ed. Francesco Donfrancesco, trans. Paola Donfrancesco (Bergamo: Moretti & Vitali, 1999). Reprinted in English in *UE* 2: *City & Soul.*

_____ (2001). "Justice and Beauty: Foundations of an Ecological Psychology," a keynote address given in Rimini, Italy, October 2001. Revised as "Justice, Beauty, and Destiny as Foundations for an Ecological Psychology," in *UE* 2: *City & Soul.*

Hough, Graham (1973). "Poetry and the Anima," *Spring: An Annual of Archetypal Psychology and Jungian Thought* (1973).

Hull, R.F.C. (1971). "Bibliographical Notes on Active Imagination in the Works of C.G. Jung," *Spring: An Annual of Archetypal Psychology and Jungian Thought* (1971).

Hulme, T.E. (1924). *Speculations* (London: Routledge, 1924).

Humbert, Elie (1971). "Active Imagination: Theory and Practice," *Spring: An Annual of Archetypal Psychology and Jungian Thought* (1971).

James, William (1909). *A Pluralistic Universe* (Lincoln: University of Nebraska Press, 1996).

Jung, Emma (1957). *Animus and Anima: Two Papers* (Putnam, Conn.: Spring Publications, 2008).

Kelly, George (1955). *The Psychology of Personal Constructs*, 2 vols. (New York: Norton, 1955).

Kugelmann, Robert (1983). *The Windows of Soul: Psychological Physiology of the Human Eye and Primary Glaucoma* (Lewisburg: Bucknell University Press, 1983).

Kugler, Paul K. (1978). "Image and Sound," *Spring: An Annual of Archetypal Psychology and Jungian Thought* (1978).

_____ (1979a). "The Phonetic Imagination," *Spring: An Annual of Archetypal Psychology and Jungian Thought* (1979).

_____ (1979b). *The Alchemy of Discourse: Image, Sound and Psyche* (Einsiedeln: Daimon, 2002).

_____, ed. (1995). *Jungian Perspectives on Clinical Supervision* (Einsiedeln: Daimon Verlag, 1995).

Leveranz, John (1979). "The Sacred Disease," *Dragonflies: Studies in Imaginal Psychology* 1 (1979).

Levinas, Emmanuel (1969). *Totality and Infinity: An Essay on Exteriority*, trans. A. Lingis (Pittsburgh: Duquesne University Press, 1969).

Lockhart, Russell A. (1977). "Cancer in Myth and Disease," *Spring: An Annual of Archetypal Psychology and Jungian Thought* (1977).

_____ (1978). "Words as Eggs," *Dragonflies: Studies in Imaginal Psychology* 1 (1978).

_____ (1980). "Psyche in Hiding," *Quadrant* 13 (1980).

López-Pedraza, Rafael (1977). *Hermes and His Children* (Einsiedeln: Daimon, 2010).

_____ (1982). "Moon Madness-Titanic Love: A Meeting of Pathology and Poetry," in *Images of the Untouched*, ed. J. Stroud and G. Thomas (Dallas: Spring Publications, 1982).

McConeghey, Howard (1981). "Art Education and Archetypal Psychology," *Spring: An Annual of Archetypal Psychology and Jungian Thought* (1981).

Meletinsky, Eleazar M. (1976). *The Poetics of Myth*, trans. G. Lanoue and A. Sadetsky (New York: Routledge, 2000).

Micklem, Niel (1979). "The Intolerable Image: The Mythic Background of Psychosis," *Spring: An Annual of Archetypal Psychology and Jungian Thought* (1979).

Miller, David L. (1972). "Polytheism and Archetypal Theology," *Journal of the American Academy of Religion* 40 (1972).

_____ (1974). *The New Polytheism: Rebirth of the Gods and Goddesses* (New York: Harper & Row, 1974).

_____ (1976a). "Fairy Tale or Myth," *Spring: An Annual of Archetypal Psychology and Jungian Thought* (1976).

_____ (1976b). "Mythopoesis, Psychopoesis, Theopoesis: The Poetries of Meaning," *Panarion Conference* tape, 1976.

_____ (1977). "Imaginings No End," *Eranos Yearbook* 46 (1977).

_____ (1981a). *Christs: Meditations on Archetypal Images in Christian Theology* (New Orleans: Spring Journal Books, 2005).

_____ (1981b). "The Two Sandals of Christ: Descent into History and into Hell," *Eranos Yearbook* 50 (1981).

Moore, Thomas (1978). "Musical Therapy," *Spring: An Annual of Archetypal Psychology and Jungian Thought* (1978).

_____ (1979a). "Artemis and the Puer," in *Puer Papers*, ed. James Hillman (Dallas: Spring Publications, 1979).

_____ (1979b). "Images in Asthma: Notes for a Study of Disease," *Dragonflies: Studies in Imaginal Psychology* 1 (1979).

_____ (1980). "James Hillman: Psychology with Soul," *Religious Studies Review* 6 (1980).

_____ (1982). *The Planets Within* (Lewisburg: Bucknell University Press, 1982).

Newman, K.D. (1980). "Counter-Transference and Consciousness," *Spring: An Annual of Archetypal Psychology and Jungian Thought* (1980).

Ogilvy, James (1977). *Many-Dimensional Man: Decentralizing Self, Society and the Sacred* (New York: Oxford University Press, 1977).

Paris, Ginette (1986). *Pagan Meditations: The Worlds of Aphrodite, Artemis, and Hestia*, trans. G. Moore (Putnam, Conn.: Spring Publications, 2005).

_____ (1990). *Pagan Grace: Dionysos, Hermes, and Goddess Memory in Daily Life*, trans. J. Mott (Putnam, Conn.: Spring Publications, 2006).

Ritsema, Rudolf (1976). "On the Syntax of the Imaginal," *Spring: An Annual of Archetypal Psychology and Jungian Thought* (1976).

Romanyshyn, Robert (1977). "Remarks on the Metaphorical Basis of Psychological Life." Paper: *First International Seminar on Archetypal Psychology*, University of Dallas, 1977.

_____ (1978–79). "Psychological Language and the Voice of Things," *Dragonflies: Studies in Imaginal Psychology* 1 (1978) and 2 (1979).

Sardello, Robert J. (1978a). "Ensouling Language," *Dragonflies: Studies in Imaginal Psychology* 1 (1978).

_____ (1978b). "An Empirical-Phenomenological Study of Fantasy," *Psychocultural Review* 2 (1978).

_____ (1979a). "Imagination and the Transformation of the Perceptual World." Paper: *Third American Conference on Fantasy and the Imaging Process*, New York, 1979.

_____ (1979b). *Educating with Soul.* Pamphlet, Center for Civic Leadership, University of Dallas, 1979.

_____ (1980a). "The Mythos of Medicine," in *Medicine and Literature: Towards a New Discipline,* ed. K.A. Rabuzzi (Baltimore: Johns Hopkins University Press, 1980).

_____ (1980b). "Beauty and Violence: The Play of Imagination in the World," *Dragonflies: Studies in Imaginal Psychology* 2 (1980).

Scott, Charles E. (1980). "On Hillman and Calvin," *Soundings* 63 (1980).

Scully, Vincent Joseph (1962). *The Earth, the Temple, and the Gods: Greek Sacred Architecture* (New Haven: Yale University Press, 1979).

Severson, Randolph (1978). "Titans Under Glass: A Recipe for the Recovery of Psychological Jargon," *Dragonflies: Studies in Imaginal Psychology* 1 (1978).

_____ (1979). "Puer's Wounded Wing: Reflections on the Psychology of Skin Disease," in *Puer Papers,* ed. James Hillman (Dallas: Spring Publications, 1979).

Simmer, Stephen (1981). "The Academy of the Dead: On Boredom, Writer's Block, Footnotes and Deadlines," *Spring: An Annual of Archetypal Psychology and Jungian Thought* (1981).

Sipiora, Michael P. (1981). "A Soul's Journey: Camus, Tuberculosis, and Aphrodite," *Spring: An Annual of Archetypal Psychology and Jungian Thought* (1981).

Stein, Murray (1973). "Hephaistos: A Pattern of Introversion," *Spring: An Annual of Archetypal Psychology and Jungian Thought* (1973).

_____ (1977). "Hera: Bound and Unbound," *Spring: An Annual of Archetypal Psychology and Jungian Thought* (1977).

Stein, Robert (1974). *Incest and Human Love* (Dallas: Spring Publications, 1984).

Vitale, Augusto (1973). "Saturn: The Transformation of the Father," in *Fathers and Mothers: Five Papers on the Archetypal Background of Family Psychology,* ed. Patricia Berry (Dallas: Spring Publications, 1990).

De Voogd, Stephanie (1977). "C.G. Jung: Psychologist of the Future, 'Philosopher' of the Past," *Spring: An Annual of Archetypal Psychology and Jungian Thought* (1977).

Watkins, Mary M. (1976). *Waking Dreams* (Putnam, Conn.: Spring Publications, 2003).

_____ (1981). "Six Approaches to the Image in Art Therapy," *Spring: An Annual of Archetypal Psychology and Jungian Thought* (1981).

Whitehead, Alfred North (1938). *Modes of Thought* (New York: The Free Press, 1968).

Wind, Edgar (1967). *Pagan Mysteries in the Renaissance* (New York: W.W. Norton, 1969).

Winquist, Charles (1981). "The Epistemology of Darkness," *Journal of the American Academy of Religion* 49 (1981).

Part Two

*Bibliography
of Archetypal Psychology*

This list is intended as a tool for those interested in archetypal psychology. Works were selected for inclusion if they are important sources for, or are clearly within the tradition of archetypal psychology. We hope to have included the most significant works of those who have published in the field.

We extend a special note of appreciation to Jessica Reiner whose un-flagging, good-humored help was indispensable for the long task of putting the original list together. Many thanks to the following people for suggestions and assistance in gathering these materials. Without them it would have immeasurably more difficult: Michael Vannoy Adams, Gustavo Barcellos, Patricia Berry, Joanne Stroud Bilby, Charles Boer, Axel Capriles, Maria Teresa Colonna, Francesco Donfrancesco, William Doty, Wolfgang Giegerich, Nor Hall, Mark Kidel, Paul Kugler, Jan Marlan, Stan Marlan, Michelle McKee, David L. Miller, Bernie Neville, Richard Olivier, Enrique Pardo, Ginette Paris, Marcus Quintaes, Monique Salzmann, Robert Sardello, Ronald Schenk, Dennis Slattery, Benjamin Sells, Luigi Turinese, Mary Watkins, Michael Whan, Emile K. Wijnans, Beverly Zabriskie, and Valery Zelensky.

– J.H.

1. *Founding Figures*

SIGMUND FREUD (b. 1856; d. 1939)

The Standard Edition of the Complete Psychological Works of Sigmund Freud,
ed. J. Strachey, 24 vols. (London: The Hogarth Press and the Institute
of Psycho-Analysis, 1953–74).

CARL GUSTAV JUNG (b. 1875; d. 1961)

Collected Works of C.G. Jung, trans. R.F.C. Hull, 20 vols. (Princeton, N.J.:
Princeton University Press, 1953–79).
Memories, Dreams, Reflection, ed. A. Jaffé; trans. R. and C. Winston (New York:
Random House, 1961).
C.G. Jung Letters, vol. 1: 1906–1950, ed. G. Adler and A. Jaffé; trans. R.F.C.
Hull; vol. 2: 1951–1960, ed. G. Adler; trans. R.F.C. Hull (Princeton,
N.J.: Princeton University Press, 1973–75).
The Freud/Jung Letters, ed. W. McGuire; trans. R. Manheim and R.F.C. Hull
(Princeton, N.J.: Princeton University Press, 1974).
Analytical Psychology: Notes of the Seminar Given in 1925, ed. W. McGuire
(Princeton, N.J.: Princeton University Press, 1989).
Dream Analysis: Notes of the Seminar Given in 1928–1930 by C.G. Jung, ed.
W. McGuire (Princeton, N.J.: Princeton University Press, 1984).
The Psychology of Kundalini Yoga: Notes of the Seminar Given in 1932 by C.G. Jung,
ed. S. Shamdasani (Princeton, N.J.: Princeton University Press, 1996).
Visions: Notes of the Seminar Given in 1930–1934 by C.G. Jung, ed. C. Douglas
(Princeton, N.J.: Princeton University Press, 1997).
Nietzsche's Zarathustra: Notes of the Seminar Given in 1934–1939 by C.G. Jung,
ed. J.L. Jarrett (Princeton, N.J.: Princeton University Press, 1988).
The Red Book: Liber Novus, ed. S. Shamdasani (New York: Norton, 2009).

HENRY CORBIN (b. 1903; d. 1978)

Alone with the Alone: Creative Imagination in the Sufism of Ibn 'Arabî, trans.
R. Manheim (Princeton, N.J.: Princeton University Press, 1998).
Avicenna and the Visionary Recital, trans. W.R. Trask (Princeton, N.J.:
Princeton University Press, 1990).
En Islam iranien: Aspects spirituels et philosophique, 4 vols. (Paris: Gallimard, 1991).
Spiritual Body and Celestial Earth: From Mazdean Iran to Shi'ite Iran, trans. N. Pearson
(Princeton, N.J.: Princeton University Press, 1989).

Le Paradoxe du monothéisme (Paris: Edition de l'Herne, 2003).
Temple and Contemplation, trans. P. and L. Sherrard (London: Kegan Paul International, 1986).
The Man of Light in Iranian Sufism, trans. N. Pearson (New Lebanon, N.Y.: Omega Publications, 1994).
An extensive bibliography can be found at *www.amiscorbin.com.*

ADOLF PORTMANN (b.1897; d.1982)

Animals as Social Beings, trans. O. Coburn (New York: Viking, 1961).
New Paths in Biology, trans. A.J. Pomerans (New York: Harper & Row, 1964).
Animal Forms and Patterns: A Study of the Appearance of Animals, trans. H. Czech; ill. S. Baur (New York: Schocken Books, 1967).
Biologie und Geist (Frankfurt am Main: Suhrkamp, 1973).
Essays in Philosophical Zoology: The Living Form and the Seeing Eye, trans. R.B. Carter (Lewiston, Penn.: Edwin Mellen, 1991).
A Zoologist Looks at Humankind, trans. J. Schaefer (New York: Columbia University Press, 1990).

JAMES HILLMAN (b.1926; d.2011)

The Uniform Edition of the Writings of James Hillman, 10 vols. (Putnam, Conn.: Spring Publications, 2004–). A complete list of published volumes can be found at *www.springpublications.com/uniformedition.html.*
Lament of the Dead: Psychology After Jung's Red Book, with Sonu Shamdasani (New York: W.W. Norton, 2013).
La Giustizia di Afrodite/Aphrodite's Justice (Capri: Edizioni La Conchiglia, 2008).
A Terrible Love of War (New York: The Penguin Press, 2004).
The Force of Character and the Lasting Life (New York: Random House, 1999).
The Soul's Code: In Search of Character and Calling (New York: Random House, 1996).
The Thought of the Heart and the Soul of the World (Putnam, Conn.: Spring Publications, 2007).
Healing Fiction (Putnam, Conn.: Spring Publications, 2009).
Anima: An Anatomy of a Personified Notion (Putnam, Conn.: Spring Publications, 2007).
Suicide and the Soul (Putnam, Conn.: Spring Publications, 2007).
Insearch: Psychology and Religion (Putnam, Conn.: Spring Publications, 2004).
Pan and the Nightmare (Putnam, Conn.: Spring Publications, 2007).
Re-Visioning Psychology (New York: Harper & Row, 1975).
The Myth of Analysis: Three Essays in Archetypal Psychology (Evanston, Ill.: Northwestern University Press, 1972).

A complete list of Hillman's publications, both in English and in translation, can be found at *www.opusarchives.org/hillman_bibliography.shtml*.

———————

The writings of the following influential scholars are too numerous to list and their bibliographies are readily available. Much of their work was first presented in lectures at the Jung Institute in Zurich and at the Eranos Conferences in Ascona. The latter lectures are to be found in the annual volumes of the *Eranos Yearbook*. The works of some of those who were presenters at these gatherings represent the "second generation" of sources for archetypal psychology and have been included in the detailed listings in Section 3 below (*Contemporary Theory and Practice*):

A. HILARY ARMSTRONG on *Neoplatonism*

JOSEPH CAMPBELL on *World Mythology*

GILBERT DURAND on *Structures of the Imagination*

MIRCEA ELIADE on *Comparative Religion*

LINDA FIERZ-DAVID on *Roman Studies*

ERIC HORNUNG on *Egyptian Religion*

TOSHIHIKO IZUTSU on *Logic of Image*

KARL KERÉNYI on *Greek Mythology*

RIVKAH SCHÄRF KLUGER on *Biblical Psychology*

JOHN LAYARD on *Anthropology and Psychology*

PAUL RADIN on *Native American Myths*

RUDOLF RITSEMA on *Imagistic Syntax*

GERSHOM SCHOLEM on *Jewish Mysticism*

HELMUTH WILHELM on *Chinese Image Thought*

MARIE-LOUISE VON FRANZ on *Fairy Tales*

2. Other Sources

Allport, Gordon W. *Becoming: Basic Considerations for a Psychology of Personality* (New Haven: Yale University Press, 1977).

Aristotle. *De Anima* and *Metaphysica,* in *The Complete Works of Aristotle,* 2 vols., ed. J. Barnes (Princeton, N.J.: Princeton University Press, 1984).

Armstrong, Robert P. *The Affecting Presence: An Essay in Humanistic Anthropology* (Urbana: University of Illinois Press, 1986).

——. *The Powers of Presence: Consciousness, Myth, and Affecting Presence* (Philadelphia: University of Pennsylvania Press, 1981).

Bachelard, Gaston. *The Psychoanalysis of Fire,* trans. by A.C.M. Ross (Boston: Beacon Press, 1968).

——. *The Poetics of Reverie: Childhood, Language, and the Cosmos,* trans. D. Russell (Boston: Beacon Press, 1971).

——. *The Poetics of Space,* trans. M. Jolas (Boston: Beacon Press, 1994).

——. *Air and Dreams: An Essay on the Imagination of Movement,* trans, E.R. and C.F. Farrell (Dallas: Dallas Institute Publications, 2002).

[A complete list of The Bachelard Translations, published by The Dallas Institute of Humanities and Culture, can be found at *www.dallasinstitute. org/books_thebachelardtranslations.html.*]

Barfield, Owen. *Poetic Diction: A Study in Meaning* (Middletown, Conn.: Wesleyan University Press, 1984).

——. *Romanticism Comes of Age: Essays on the Creative Imagination* (Oxford: Barfield Press UK, 2012).

——. *What Coleridge Thought* (Oxford: Barfield Press UK, 2006).

——. *The Rediscovery of Meaning and Other Essays* (Oxford: Barfield Press UK, 2006).

——. *Saving the Appearances: A Study in Idolatry* (Middletown, Conn.: Wesleyan University Press, 1988).

Bergson, Henri. *Creative Evolution,* trans. A. Mitchell (London: Palgrave Macmillan, 2007).

Bodkin, Maud. *Archetypal Patterns in Poetry: Psychological Studies of Imagination* (London: Oxford University Press, 1963).

Brown, Norman O. *Closing Time* (New York: Random House, 1973).

Coleridge, Samuel Taylor. *The Collected Works of Samuel Taylor Coleridge,* 23 vols. (Princeton: N.J.: Princeton University Press, 1969–).

Dodds, E.R. *The Greeks and the Irrational* (Berkeley: University of California Press, 2004).

Eliot, T.S. *The Complete Poems and Plays: 1909–1950* (New York: Houghton Mifflin Harcourt, 1971).

Ficino, Marsilio. *The Book of Life,* trans. C. Boer (Dallas: Spring Publications, 1980).

———. *Commentary on Plato's Symposium on Love,* ed. and trans. S. Jayne (Woodstock, Conn.: Spring Publications, 1985).

Friedlander, Paul. *Plato,* trans. H. Meyerhof, 3 vols. (Princeton, N.J.: Princeton University Press, 1958–69).

Frye, Northrop. *The Anatomy of Criticism: Four Essays* (Princeton, N.J.: Princeton University Press, 2000).

Gibson, J.J. *The Perception of the Visual World* (Boston: Houghton Mifflin, 1950).

———. *The Ecological Approach to Visual Perception* (Hillsdale, N.J.: Lawrence Erlbaum Associates, 1989).

Guénon, René. *The Reign of Quantity & the Signs of the Times* (Hillsdale, N.Y.: Sophia Perennis, 2001).

Heraclitus. Greek text with commentary by M. Marcovich (Merida, Venezuela: Los Andes University Press, 1967).

Hulme, T.E. *Speculations: Essays on Humanism and the Philosophy of Art,* ed. H. Read (London: Routledge, 1924).

James, William. *A Pluralistic Universe* and *Pragmatism,* in *Writings 1902–1910,* ed. B. Kuklick (New York: Library of America, 1988).

Jaspers, Karl. *General Psychopathology,* trans J. Hoenig and M.W. Hamilton, 2 vols. (Baltimore: The Johns Hopkins University Press, 1997).

Joyce, James. *Ulysses* (New York: Modern Library, 1992).

———. *The Restored Finnegans Wake,* ed. D. Rose and J. O'Hanlon (London: Penguin Classics, 2012).

Jung, Emma. *Animus and Anima: Two Papers* (Putnam, Conn.: Spring Publications, 2008).

Keats, John. *Poetical Works* (Oxford: Clarendon Press, 1958).

Kelly, George. *The Psychology of Personal Constructs,* 2 vols. (New York: Norton, 1955).

Klein, Yves. *Overcoming the Problematics of Art: The Writings of Yves Klein,* trans. K. Ottmann (Putnam, Conn.: Spring Publications, 2007).

Klibansky, Raymond, Irwin Panofsky, and Fritz Saxl. *Saturn and Melancholy: Studies in the History of Natural Philosophy, Religion, and Art* (New York: Basic Books, 1964).

Kristeller, Paul Oskar. *The Philosophy of Marsilio Ficino,* trans. V. Conant (Gloucester, Mass.: Peter Smith, 1964).

Levinas, Emmanuel. *Totality and Infinity,* trans. A. Lingis (Pittsburgh: Duquesne University Press, 1969).

Lévy-Bruhl, Lucien. *The Soul of the Primitive,* trans. L.A. Clare (London: George Allen & Unwin, 1965).

——. *How Natives Think,* trans. L.A. Clare (Princeton, N.J.: Princeton University Press, 1985).

Makkreel, Rudolf A. *Dilthey: Philosopher of Human Studies* (Princeton, N.J.: Princeton University Press, 1992).

Mann, Thomas. *Doctor Faustus,* trans. J.E. Woods (New York: Vintage, 1999).

Marcel, Raymond. *Marsile Ficin, 1433–1499* (Paris: Société d'édition les belles lettres, 1958).

Meier, C.A. *Healing Dream and Ritual: Ancient Incubation and Modern Psychotherapy* (Einsiedeln: Daimon, 2012).

Merleau-Ponty, Maurice. *The Visible and the Invisible,* trans. A. Lingis (Evanston, Ill.: Northwestern University Press, 1969).

Onians, R.B. *The Origins of European Thought About the Body, the Mind, the Soul, the World, Time, and Fate* (Cambridge: Cambridge University Press, 1988).

Otto, Walter F. *The Homeric Gods: The Spiritual Significance of Greek Religion,* trans. M. Hadas (London: Thames & Hudson, 1979).

——. *Dionysus, Myth and Cult,* trans. R.B. Palmer (Dallas: Spring Publications, 1981).

Pepper, Stephen C. *World Hypotheses: A Study in Evidence* (Berkeley: University of California Press, 1942).

The Collected Dialogues of Plato, Including the Letters, ed. E. Hamilton and H. Cairns (Princeton, N.J.: Princeton University Press, 1961).

Plotinus. *The Enneads,* trans. A.H. Armstrong (Cambridge, Mass.: Harvard University Press, 1966).

Polti, Georges. *The Thirty-Six Dramatic Situations,* trans. L. Rey (Franklin, Ohio: James Knapp Reeve, 1921).

Propp, Vladimir. *Morphology of the Folktale,* trans. L. Scott (Austin: University of Texas Press, 1968).

Raine, Kathleen. *Blake and Tradition,* 2 vols. (London: Routledge & Kegan Paul, 1969).

Raine, Kathleen and George M. Harper, eds. *Thomas Taylor the Platonist: Selected Writings* (Princeton, N.J.: Princeton University Press, 1969).

Rohde, Erwin. *Psyche: The Cult of Souls and Belief in Immortality Among the Greeks,* trans. W. B. Hillis (London: Routledge & Kegan Paul, 1925).

Santayana, George. *Skepticism and Animal Faith: Introduction to a System of Philosophy* (New York: Dover, 1955).

Scholem, Gershom, *Alchemy & Kabbalah,* trans. K. Ottmann (Putnam, Conn.: Spring Publications, 2006).

Seznec, Jean. *The Survival of the Pagan Gods: The Mythological Tradition and Its Place in Renaissance Humanism and Art*, trans. B.F. Sessions (Princeton, N.J.: Princeton University Press, 1953).

The Chief Works of Benedict de Spinoza, trans. R.H.M. Elwes, 2 vols. (London: G. Bell and Sons, 1883–84).

Stevens, Wallace. *Collected Poems* (New York: Knopf, 1964).

Tagliacozzo, Giorgio and Donald Phillip Verene (eds.). *Giambattista Vico's Science of Humanity* (Baltimore: The Johns Hopkins University Press, 1976).

Thompson, Stith. *The Folktale* (Berkeley: University of California Press, 1977).

Vico, Giambattista. *The New Science*, trans. D. Marsh (Harmondsworth: Penguin, 1999).

Von Beit, Hedwig and Marie-Louise von Franz. *Symbolik des Märchens*, 3 vols. (Bern: Francke, 1952).

Whitehead, Alfred North. *Modes of Thought* (New York: The Free Press, 1968).

Wind, Edgar. *Pagan Mysteries in the Renaissance* (New York: Norton, 1968).

Yates, Frances A. *The Art of Memory* (London: Pimlico, 2007).

The Collected Poems of W.B. Yeats, ed. R.F. Finneran (New York: Scribner, 1996).

3. Contemporary Theory and Practice

A. *Journals*

Anima, ed. Francesco Donfrancesco (Florence, Italy, since 1988).

Dragonflies: Studies in Imaginal Psychology, ed. Robert Sardello (Irving, Texas, 1978–1980).

Gorgo: Zeitschrift für archetypische Psychologie und bildhaftes Denken, ed. Allan Guggenbühl (Zurich, Switzerland, 1980–2008).

L'immaginale: Rassegna di psicologia immaginale, ed. Loredana Benvenga (Lecce, Italy, since 1983).

Mythosphere: A Journal for Image, Myth and Symbol, ed. William G. Doty (Tuscaloosa, Alabama, 1994–2001).

Novaya Vesna (New Spring): Annual Almanac of Post-Jungian Psychology and Culture, ed. Valery Zelensky (St. Petersburg, Russia, since 1991).

Rivista di Psicologia Analitica, ed. Marcello Pignatelli (Rome, Italy, since 1970).

Salt Journal, ed. David Barton (San Marcos, Texas, 1997–2001).

Sphinx: A Journal for Archetypal Psychology and the Arts, ed. Noel Cobb and Eva Loewe (London, 1988–1996).

Spring: A Magazine of Jungian Thought (1941–59; 1960–61); *Spring: Contributions to Jungian Thought* (1962–69); *Spring: An Annual of Archetypal Psychology and Jungian Thought* (1970–87); *Spring: A Journal of Archetype and Culture* (since 1988); various editors. *Spring* has been indexed twice: 1941–79 in *Spring Index* by V. Detloff (1983), and 1970–94 in *Spring: A Journal of Archetype and Culture* 56 (1998).

Sulfur: A Literary Bi-Annual of the Whole Art, ed. Clayton Eshleman (Ypsilanti, Michigan, 1981–2000).

I quaderni di Yseos (Acireale, Italy, since 1998).

B. *Books and Articles*

Abram, David. *The Spell of the Sensuous: Perception and Language in a More-Than-Human World* (New York: Vintage Books, 1997).

Adams, Michael Vannoy. "Deconstructive Philosophy and Imaginal Psychology: Comparative Perspectives on Jacques Derrida and James Hillman," in *Jungian Literary Criticism*, ed. R.P. Sugg (Evanston, Ill.: Northwestern University Press, 1992).

———. "Flowers and Fungi: Archetypal Semiotics and Visual Metaphor," *Spring: A Journal of Archetype and Culture* 59 (1996).

———. *The Multicultural Imagination: Race, Color, and the Unconscious* (London: Routledge, 1996).

———. "Metaphors in Psychoanalytic Theory and Therapy," *Clinical Social Work Journal* 25, no. 1 (1997).

———. "Refathering Psychoanalysis: Deliteralising Hillman: Imaginal Therapy, Individual and Cultural," in *On the Sublime in Psychoanalysis, Archetypal Psychology, and Psychotherapy*, ed. P. Clarkson (below).

———. "Desegregating the White Ego: Racism and the Ethic of White Civilization," *Spring: A Journal of Archetype and Culture* 62 (1997).

———. "For Love of the Imagination," in *Why I Became a Psychotherapist*, ed. J. Reppen (Northvale, N.J., and London: Jason Aronson, 1998).

———. "Compensation in the Service of Individuation: Phenomenological Essentialism and Jungian Dream Interpretation," *Psychoanalytic Dialogues* 10, no. 1 (2000).

———. "Mythological Knowledge: Just How Important Is It in Jungian (and Freudian) Analysis?" *Harvest* 48, no. 1 (2002).

———. "The Archetypal School," in *The Cambridge Companion to Jung*, ed. P. Young-Eisendrath and T. Dawson (below).

———. "Imaginology: The Jungian Study of the Imagination," in *Archetypal Psychologies: Reflections in Honor of James Hillman*, ed. S. Marlan (below).

———. *The Mythological Unconscious* (Putnam, Conn.: Spring Publications, 2010).

Aizenstaat, Stephen. "Jungian Psychology and the World Unconscious," in *Ecopsychology*, ed. T. Roszak, M.E. Gomes and A.D. Kanner (San Francisco: Sierra Club, 1995).

Andrews, Valerie, R. Bosnak, and K. Goodwin, eds. *Facing Apocalypse* (Putnam, Conn.: Spring Publications, 2004).

Armstrong, A.H. "Some Advantages of Polytheism," *Dionysius* 5 (1981).

———. *On Beauty* (Dallas: Spring Publications, 1987).

Avens, Roberts. *Imagination Is Reality: Western Nirvana in Jung, Hillman, Barfield, and Cassirer* (Putnam, Conn.: Spring Publications, 2003).

———. "James Hillman: Towards a Poetic Psychology," *Journal of Religion and Health* 19, no. 3 (1980).

———. "Heidegger and Archetypal Psychology," *International Philosophical Quarterly* 22 (1982).

———. *Imaginal Body: Para-Jungian Reflections on Soul, Imagination, and Death* (Washington, D.C.: University Press of America, 1982).

———. *The New Gnosis* (Putnam, Conn.: Spring Publications, 2006).

Baeten, Elizabeth M. *The Magic Mirror: Myth's Abiding Power* (Albany: State University of New York Press, 1996).

Barasch, Marc Ian. *The Healing Path: A Soul Approach to Illness* (New York: Penguin, 1994).

Barcellos, Gustavo. "Anima 30 anos Pós-Jung," in J. Hillman, *Psicologia arquetípica* (São Paulo: Cultrix, 1992).

———. "Classics Revisited: *The Waste Land* at Century's End," *The San Francisco Jung Institute Library Journal* 18, no. 1 (1999).

South and Archetypal Psychology: The Brazilian Experience," in *Psychology at the Threshold*, ed. D.P. Slattery and L. Corbett (below).

———. *Vôos & raízes: ensaios sobre psicologia arquetípica, imaginação e arte* (São Paulo: Editora Ágora, 2006).

Barnaby, Karin and Pellegrino D'Acierno. *C.G. Jung and the Humanities: Toward a Hermeneutics of Culture* (Princeton, N.J.: Princeton University Press, 1990).

Bedford, Gary S. "Notes on Mythological Psychology," *Journal of the American Academy of Religion* 49 (1981).

Beebe, John, ed. *Terror, Violence and the Impulse to Destroy: Perspectives from Analytical Psychology* (Einsiedeln: Daimon Verlag, 2012).

Berry, Patricia. *Echo's Subtle Body: Contributions to an Archetypal Psychology* (Putnam, Conn.: Spring Publications, 2008).

———. "Some Dream Motifs Accompanying the 'Abandonment' of an Analytical Practice," *Chiron: A Review of Jungian Analysis* (1985).

———, ed. *Fathers and Mothers* (Dallas: Spring Publications, 1990).

———. "Light and Shadow," in *The Shadow in America: Reclaiming the Soul of a Nation*, ed. J. Abrams (Novato, Calif.: Nataraj Publishing, 1994).

———. "Reductionism /Finding the Child," in *Fire in the Stone: The Alchemy of Desire*, ed. S. Marlan (below).

———. "Image in Motion," in *Jung & Film: Post-Jungian Takes on the Moving Image*, ed. C. Hauke and I. Alister (Philadelphia: Taylor & Francis, 2001).

Bishop, Peter. *The Myth of Shangri-La: Tibet, Travel Writing, and the Western Creation of Sacred Landscape* (Berkeley: University of California Press, 1989).

———. *The Greening of Psychology: The Vegetable World in Myth, Dream, and Healing* (Dallas: Spring Publications, 1990).

———. *Dreams of Power: Tibetan Buddhism and the Western Imagination* (Rutherford, N.J.: Fairleigh Dickinson University Press, 1993).

———. *An Archetypal Constable: National Identity and the Geography of Nostalgia* (Madison, N.J.: Fairleigh Dickinson University Press, 1995).

Blakeslee, Mermer. *In the Yikes! Zone: A Conversation with Fear* (New York: Dutton, 2002).

Bleakley, Alan. *Earth's Embrace: Archetypal Psychology's Challenge to the Growth Movement* (Bath: Gateway Books, 1989).

——. "Greens and Greenbacks," *Spring: A Journal of Archetype and Culture* 52 (1992).

——. "Psychotherapy Stinks! – or Hekate Rising," *Sphinx: Journal for Archetypal Psychology and the Arts* 7 (1996).

——. "The Violent Claims of Red Sulphur: Cultural Readings through Alchemical Psychology," *Harvest: Journal for Jungian Studies* 44, no. 2 (1998).

——. *The Animalizing Imagination: Totemism, Textuality and Ecocriticism* (London: Palgrave Macmillan, 2000).

Bly, Robert. *A Little Book on the Human Shadow* (San Francisco: Harper & Row, 1988).

——. *Iron John: A Book About Men* (Cambridge, Mass.: Da Capo Press, 2004).

——. *The Sibling Society* (New York: Addison-Wesley, 1996).

Bly, Robert, James Hillman, and Michael Meade, eds. *The Rag and Bone Shop of the Heart: Poems for Men* (San Francisco: Harper Perennial, 1993).

Bly, Robert and Marion Woodman. *The Maiden King: The Reunion of Masculine and Feminine* (New York: Henry Holt, 1998).

Boer, Charles (trans.) *The Homeric Hymns* (Dallas: Spring Publications, 1979).

——. "Poetry and Psyche," *Spring: An Annual of Archetypal Psychology and Jungian Thought* (1979).

——. "In the Shadow of the Gods: Greek Tragedy," *Spring: A Journal of Archetype and Culture* (1982).

——, trans. *Ovid's Metamorphoses* (Dallas: Spring Publications, 1989).

——. "Canonization/Decanonization/Recanonization," *Spring: A Journal of Archetype and Culture* 51 (1991).

——. "The Classicist and the Psychopath," in W.B. Stanford, *The Ulysses Theme* (Dallas: Spring Publications, 1992).

——. "A Preface," in K. Kerényi, *Hermes: Guide of Souls* (Woodstock, Conn.: Spring Publications, 1995).

——. "Watch Your Step," *Spring: A Journal of Archetype and Culture* 59 (1996).

——. "Confessions of an Altar Boy," *The Salt Journal* 2, no. 5 (2000).

——. "Honey, I Swear I Don't Have Hermes," *Spring: A Journal of Archetype and Culture* 67 (2000).

Boer, Charles and James Hillman. *Freud's Own Cookbook* (New York: Harper Collins, 1985).

Boer, Charles and Peter Kugler. "Archetypal Psychology is Mythical Realism," *Spring: An Annual of Archetypal Psychology and Jungian Thought* (1977).

Bosnak, Robert. "The Dirty Needle: Images of the Inferior Analyst," *Spring: An Annual of Archetypal Psychology and Jungian Thought* (1984).

———. *Tracks in the Wilderness of Dreaming: Exploring Interior Landscape Through Practical Dreamwork* (New York: Delacorte Press, 1996).

———. "Integration and Ambivalence in Transplants," in *Trauma and Dreams*, ed. D. Barrett (Cambridge, Mass.: Harvard University Press, 1996).

———. *A Little Course in Dreams* (Boston: Shambhala, 1997).

———. *Christopher's Dreams: Dreaming and Living with AIDS* (New York: Delta, 1997).

Bregman, Lucy. "Religious Imagination: Polytheistic Psychology Confronts Calvin," *Soundings* 63 (1980).

Brooke, Roger. *Jung and Phenomenology* (Amherst, N.Y.: Trivium, 2009).

———, ed. *Pathways into the Jungian World: Phenomenology and Analytical Psychology* (London: Routledge, 1999).

Calasso, Roberto. *The Marriage of Cadmus and Harmony*, trans. T. Parks (New York: Vintage, 1994).

———. *Literature and the Gods*, trans. T. Parks (New York: Vintage, 2001).

Capriles, Axel. "Psicohistoria o la Reaparición de Mnemosine," *Eidos* 1, no. 3 (1984).

———. "Entre Ciencia y Literatura: El psicoanálisis como lectura de imágenes," *Boletín universitario de letras* 1 (1993).

———. "La Cultura Empresarial como Cultura Desapasionada," *Revista Montalban* 26 (1994).

———. *El complejo del dinero* (Caracas: Ediciones BXEL, 1996).

Ann Casement, ed. *Post-Jungians Today: Key Papers in Contemporary Analytical Psychology* (London and New York: Routledge, 1998).

Casey, Edward S. "Toward an Archetypal Imagination," *Spring: An Annual of Archetypal Psychology and Jungian Thought* (1974).

———. "Time in the Soul," *Spring: An Annual of Archetypal Psychology and Jungian Thought* (1979).

———. "Getting Placed: Soul in Space," *Spring: An Annual of Archetypal Psychology and Jungian Thought* (1982).

———. *The Fate of Place: A Philosophical History* (Berkeley: University of California Press, 1997).

———. *Imagining: A Phenomenological Study* (Bloomington: Indiana University Press, 2000).

———. *Remembering: A Phenomenological Study* (Bloomington: Indiana University Press, 2000).

———. *Representing Place: Landscape Painting and Maps* (Minneapolis: University of Minnesota Press, 2002).

———. *Spirit and Soul: Essays in Philosophical Psychology* (Putnam, Conn.: Spring Publications, 2004).

——. *Earth-Mapping: Artists Reshaping Landscape* (Minneapolis: University of Minnesota Press, 2005).

——. *Getting Back into Place: Toward a Renewed Understanding of the Place-World* (Bloomington: Indiana University Press, 2009).

Cazenave, Michel, ed. *Science and Consciousness: Two Views of the Universe*, trans. A. Hall and E. Callander (Oxford: Pergamon Press, 1984).

Chapelle, Daniel. *Nietzsche and Psychoanalysis* (Albany, N.Y.: State University of New York Press, 1993).

Cheetham, Tom. "Dogmas, Idols and the Edge of Chaos," *Human Ecology Review* 7, no. 1 (2000).

——. "Consuming Passions: The Stars, the Feast, and the Science of the Balance," *Temenos Academy Review* 5 (2002).

——. "Within This Darkness: Incarnation, Theophany, and the Primordial Revelation," *Esoterica: The Journal for Esoteric Studies* IV (2002).

——. *The World Turned Inside Out: Henry Corbin and Islamic Mysticism* (Woodstock, Conn.: Spring Journal Books, 2003).

——. *Green Man, Earth Angel: The Prophetic Tradition and the Battle for the Soul of the World* (Albany, N.Y.: State University of New York Press, 2004).

——. *After Prophecy: Imagination, Incarnation, and the Unity of the Prophetic Tradition* (New Orleans: Spring Journal Books, 2007).

——. *All the World an Icon: Henry Corbin and the Angelic Function of Beings* (Berkeley: North Atlantic Books, 2012)

Christou, Evangelos. *The Logos of the Soul* (Putnam, Conn.: Spring Publications, 2007).

Clarkson, Petrūska, ed. *On the Sublime in Psychoanalysis, Archetypal Psychology, and Psychotherapy* (London: Whurr Publishers, 1997).

Cobb, Noel. *Prospero's Island: The Secret Alchemy at the Heart of The Tempest* (London: Coventure, 1990).

——. "Who Is Behind Archetypal Psychology?" *Spring: An Annual of Archetypal Psychology and Jungian Thought* (1988).

——. "The Fires of Eros and the Alchemy of Seduction," *Sphinx: Journal for Archetypal Psychology and the Arts* 3 (1990).

——. *Archetypal Imagination: Glimpses of the Gods in Life and Art* (Hudson, N.Y.: Lindisfarne Press, 1992).

——. "Working with Gold: The Mozartian Jewels of Kevin Coates," *Sphinx: Journal for Archetypal Psychology and the Arts* 4 (1992).

——. "Anima Socialis: The Soul of the Convivium," *Sphinx: Journal for Archetypal Psychology and the Arts* 6 (1994).

——. "On Archetypal Psychology's Missing Alchemical Marriage. Part One: Red King Proposes to White Queen," *Sphinx: Journal for Archetypal Psychology and the Arts* 7 (1996).

Colilli, Paul. *The Idea of a Living Spirit: Poetic Logic as a Contemporary Theory* (Toronto: University of Toronto Press, 1997).

Colonna, Maria Teresa. "Il mondo infero e la coscienza," *Rivista di Psicologia Analitica* 31 (1985).

———. "Dolore e sofferenza dell'analista," *Rivista di Psicologia Analitica* 36 (1987).

———. "L'incertezza sui sogni," *Rivista di Psicologia Analitica* 43 (1991).

———. "La condizione postmoderna: l'esilio degli Dei," *Rivista di Psicologia Analitica* 56 (1997).

———. "Fantasie e riflessioni sull'arte di un post-junghiano," *Rivista di Psicologia Analitica* 59 (1999).

———. "Grandi domande e risposte del nostro tempo," *Rivista di Psicologia Analitica* 61 (2000).

———. "L'ultima età della vita e le sue immagini," *Rivista di Psicologia Analitica* 62 (2000).

———. "Psicoanalisi e cinema. L'origine di una vocazione," *Rivista di Psicologia Analitica* 63 (2001).

Cousineau, Phil, ed. *Soul: An Archaeology. Readings From Socrates to Ray Charles* (San Francisco: Harper, 1994).

Cowan, Lyn. "On Masochism," *Spring: An Annual of Archetypal Psychology and Jungian Thought* (1979).

———. *Masochism: A Jungian View* (Dallas: Spring Publications, 1982).

———. *Tracking the White Rabbit: Essays in Subversive Psychology* (London: Brunner-Routledge, 2002).

David, Julian. "Discussion on Jung and Hillman," *Harvest: Journal for Jungian Studies* 31 (1985).

Davis, Robert H. *Jung, Freud, and Hillman: Three Depth Psychologies in Context* (Westport, Conn., and London: Praeger, 2003).

Donfrancesco, Antonietta. "La perdita come possibilità d'interezza," *Anima* (1998).

———. "La coscienza radicata in Anima," *I quaderni di Yseos* (1998).

———. "La felicità. Un sentimento possibile," *I quaderni di Yseos* (1999).

———. "Il corpo pensoso," *I quaderni di Yseos* (2000).

Donfrancesco, Francesco. "James Hillman e il mondo immaginale," in *Psicologia analitica contemporanea*, ed. C. Trombetta (Milano: Bompiani, 1989).

———. "Mimesis," *Harvest: Journal for Jungian Studies* 41 (1995).

———. *Nello specchio di Psiche* (Bergamo: Moretti & Vitali, 1996).

———. *L'artefice silenziosa e la ricostruzione di uno spazio interiore* (Bergamo: Moretti & Vitali, 1998).

———. "The Longing for a Mentor," *Spring: A Journal of Archetype and Culture* 63 (1998).

———. *No espelho de Psique* (São Paulo: Paulus, 2000).

———, ed. *Un oscuro impulso interiore* (Bergamo: Moretti & Vitali, 2000).

———. Life Inside Death: Through the Art of Zoran Music," *Harvest: Journal for Jungian Studies* 46 (2000).

———. *Una poetica dell'analisi* (Bergamo: Moretti & Vitali, 2000).

———, ed. *Per nascosti sentieri* (Bergamo: Moretti & Vitali, 2001).

———. "The Care of Art," in *Cambridge 2001: Proceedings of the 15th International Congress for Analytical Psychology*, ed. M.A. Mattoon (Einsiedeln: Daimon Verlag, 2002).

———. *Pensare l'anima* (Bergamo: Moretti & Vitali, 2008).

———, ed. *James Hillman: Verso il sapere dell'anima* (Bergamo: Moretti & Vitali, 2012).

Doty, William. *Mythography: The Study of Myths and Rituals* (Tuscaloosa: University of Alabama Press, 2000).

Drob, Sanford. "The Depth of Soul: James Hillman's Vision of Psychology," *Journal of Humanistic Psychology* 39, no. 3 (1999).

Duncan, Robert. "Opening the Dreamway" and "Wind and Sea, Fire and Night," *Spring: A Journal of Archetype and Culture* 59 (1996).

Frabotta, Biancamaria, ed. *Arcipelago malinconia: scenari e parole dell'interiorità* (Rome: Donzelli, 2001).

Freedberg, David. *The Power of Images: Studies in the History and Theory of Response* (Chicago: University of Chicago Press, 1989).

Frey-Wehrlin, C.T., R. Bosnak, et al. "The Treatment of Chronic Psychosis," *Journal of Analytical Psychology* 23 (1978).

Garufi, Bianca. "Reflections on the 'rêve éveillé dirigé' method," *Journal of Analytical Psychology* 22 (1977).

———. "Sul preconcetto di inferiorità della donna," *Rivista di Psicologia Analitica* 16 (1977).

———. "La moda come relazione corpo-psiche," *Rivista di Psicologia Analitica* 23 (1981).

———. "L'interpretazione innata," *Anima* (1990).

———. "Un esempio di funzione trascendente," *Rivista di Psicologia Analitica* 43 (1991).

———. "Reale e surreale. Note fra sogno e veglia," *Anima* (1991).

———. "Anima Mundi and Anima Mater: A Reply to James Hillman's Views on the Narcissism of Psychology," *Sphinx: A Journal for Archetypal Psychology and the Arts* 5 (1993).

———. "Sull'immagine," *Rivista di Psicologia Analitica* 50 (1994).

———. "L'assassino interiore," *Anima* (1996).

———. "La Street Art a New York negli anni '80: Un ricordo personale," *Rivista di Psicologia Analitica* 59 (1999).

Gary, Richard M. *Archetypal Explorations: Towards an Archetypal Sociology* (New York: Routledge, 1996).

Gehrts, Heino, Wolfgang Giegerich, Hellmut Haug, Ulrich Mann, Anita von Raffay, and Viktor Zielen. "Polytheismus-Diskussion," *Gorgo* 2 (1979).

Gibson, Karen, Donald Lathrop, and E. Mark Stern, eds. *Carl Jung and Soul Psychology* (New York: Hawarth, 1991).

Giegerich, Wolfgang. "On the Neurosis of Psychology or the Third of the Two," *Spring: An Annual of Archetypal Psychology and Jungian Thought* (1977).

———. "Buße für Philemon: Vertiefung in das verdorbene Gast-Spiel der Götter," *Eranos Yearbook* 51 (1982).

———. "The Nuclear Bomb and the Fate of God," *Spring: An Annual of Archetypal Psychology and Jungian Thought* (1985).

———. "The Invention of Explosive Power and the Blueprint of the Bomb: A Chapter in the Imaginal Pre-History of Our Nuclear Predicament," *Spring: An Annual of Archetypal Psychology and Jungian Thought* (1988).

———. "Deliverance from the Stream of Events: Okeanos and the Circulation of the Blood," *Sulfur* 21 (Winter 1988).

———. "Ending Emancipation from History: Kafka's 'In the Penal Colony,'" *Sulfur* 37 (Fall 1995).

———. "Is the Soul 'Deep'? Entering and Following the Logical Movement of Heraclitus' 'Fragment 45,'" *Spring: A Journal of Archetype and Culture* 64 (1998).

———. "The 'Patriarchal Neglect of the Feminine Principle': A Psychological Fallacy in Jungian Theory," *Harvest: Journal for Jungian Studies* 45, no. 1 (1999).

———. *The Soul's Logical Life: Towards a Rigorous Notion of Psychology* (New York: Peter Lang, 1999).

———, David L. Miller, and Greg Mogenson, *Dialectics and Analytical Psychology: The El Capitan Canyon Seminar* (New Orleans: Spring Journal Books, 2005).

———. *The Collected English Papers of Wolfgang Giegerich*, 4 vols. (New Orleans: Spring Journal Books, 2005–10).

———. *What Is Soul?* (New Orleans: Spring Journal Books, 2012).

Goldenberg, Naomi. "Archetypal Theory after Jung," *Spring: An Annual of Archetypal Psychology and Jungian Thought* (1975).

———. *Changing of the Gods: Feminism and the End of Traditional Religion* (Boston: Beacon Press, 1979).

———. "A Critique of 'Psyche' in the Work of James Hillman," *Anima* 11, no. 2 (1985).

———. *Resurrecting the Body: Feminism, Religion and Psychotherapy* (New York: Crossroad, 1993).

Griffin, David Ray, ed. *Archetypal Process: Self and Divine in Whitehead, Jung, and Hillman* (Evanston, Ill.: Northwestern University Press, 1989).

Grinnell, Robert. "Reflections on the Archetype of Consciousness: Personality and Psychological Faith," *Spring: An Annual of Archetypal Psychology and Jungian Thought* (1970).

——. "In Praise of the 'Instinct for Unholiness': Intimations of a Moral Archetype," *Spring: An Annual of Archetypal Psychology and Jungian Thought* (1971).

——. *Alchemy in a Modern Woman* (Zurich: Spring Publications, 1973).

Guggenbühl, Allan. *The Incredible Fascination of Violence: Dealing With Aggression and Brutality Among Children*, trans. Julia Hillman (Woodstock, Conn.: Spring Publications, 1996).

——. *Men, Power, and Myths: The Quest for Male Identity*, trans. G.V. Hartman (New York: Continuum, 1997).

Guggenbühl-Craig, Adolf. "Must Analysis Fail Through Its Destructive Aspect?" *Spring: An Annual of Archetypal Psychology and Jungian Thought* (1970).

——. "Analytical Rigidity and Ritual," *Spring: An Annual of Archetypal Psychology and Jungian Thought* (1972).

——. "The Archetype of the Invalid and the Limits of Healing," *Spring: An Annual of Archetypal Psychology and Jungian Thought* (1979).

"The Demonic Side of Sexuality," in *Meeting the Shadow*, ed. C. Zweig and J. Abrams (below).

——. *Marriage Is Dead – Long Live Marriage!* trans. M. Stein (formerly *Marriage: Dead or Alive*) (Putnam, Conn.: Spring Publications, 2008).

——. *The Old Fool and the Corruption of Myth*, trans. D. Wilson (Putnam, Conn.: Spring Publications, 2006).

——. *From the Wrong Side: A Paradoxical Approach to Psychology*, ed. and trans. G.V. Hartman (Woodstock, Conn.: Spring Publications, 1995).

——. *Power in the Helping Professions*, trans. M. Gubitz (Putnam, Conn.: Spring Publications, 2009).

——. *The Emptied Soul: On the Nature of the Psychopath*, trans. G.V. Hartman (formerly *Eros on Crutches*) (Putnam, Conn.: Spring Publications, 2008).

Hall, James A. "Differences between Jung and Hillman," in *Essays on Jung and the Study of Religion*, ed. L.H. Martin and J. Goss (Lanham, Md.: University Press of America, 1985).

Hall, Nor. *Mothers and Daughters* (Minneapolis: Rusoff Books, 1976).

——. *The Moon and the Virgin: Reflections on the Archetypal Feminine* (New York: Harper Perennial, 1980).

——. *Those Women* (Dallas: Spring Publications, 1988).

——. *Broodmales* (Dallas: Spring Publications, 1989).

——. "Maenads: Mad Matrons and Meditative Maidens," *Sphinx: A Journal for Archetypal Psychology and the Arts* 2 (1989).

————. "Changing the Subject: Behind the Scenes in Psychotherapy's Theatre," *Sphinx: A Journal for Archetypal Psychology and the Arts* 4 (1992).

————. "Behind the Scenes in Therapy," in *Nourishing the Soul: Discovering the Sacred in Everyday Life*, ed. Anne A. Simpkinson, Charles H. Simpkinson, and Rose Solari (San Francisco: Harper, 1995).

————. "A Collage that Spoke," *Spring: A Journal of Archetype and Culture* 59 (1996).

————. "Daughters of Memory," *The Open Page*, No. 1 (January 1996).

————. "Architecture of Intimacy," *Spring: A Journal of Archetype and Culture* 60 (1996).

————. "Vanishing Writing: Collaborative Text Development for Non-Text-Based Theatre," *The Open Page*, No. 6 (March 2001).

————. *Irons in the Fire* (Barrytown, N.Y.: Station Hill Press, 2002).

————, with Harriet Bart and Laura Crosby. *Traces* (Minneapolis: Ohm Editions, 2010).

Hampden-Turner, Charles. *Maps of the Mind: Charts and Concepts of the Mind and its Labyrinths* (New York: Macmillan, 1982).

Harpur, Patrick. *The Philosopher's Secret Fire: A History of the Imagination* (London: Penguin Books, 2002).

Hartman, Gary V. "Psychotherapy: An Attempt at Definition," *Spring: An Annual of Archetypal Psychology and Jungian Thought* (1980).

Hauke, Christopher. *Jung and the Postmodern: The Interpretation of Realities* (London: Routledge, 2000).

Hawkins, Ernest. "On Migraine: From Dionysos to Freud," *Dragonflies: Studies in Imaginal Psychology* 1, no. 2 (1979).

Higuchi, Kazuhiko. "Necessity of Beauty: 'Death Poems – Dying in Beauty,'" *Psicologia dinamica* (1997).

Hough, Graham. "Poetry and the Anima," *Spring: An Annual of Archetypal Psychology and Jungian Thought* (1973).

Hoy, Daniel J. "Hillman/Jung: Toward Bridging the Chasm of Oppositions," *Harvest: Journal for Jungian Studies* 31 (1985).

Humbert, Elie. "Active Imagination: Theory and Practice," *Spring: An Annual of Archetypal Psychology and Jungian Thought* (1971).

Kawai, Hayao. *The Japanese Psyche: Major Motifs in the Fairy Tales of Japan*, trans. H. Kawai and S. Reece (Dallas: Spring Publications, 1988).

————. *The Buddhist Priest Myoē: A Life of Dreams*, trans. M. Unno (Venice, Calif.: Lapis Press, 1992).

————. *Dreams, Myths, and Fairy Tales in Japan* (Einsiedeln: Daimon Verlag, 1995).

————. *Buddhism and the Art of Psychotherapy* (College Station: Texas A&M University Press, 1996).

Kearney, Michael. *A Place of Healing: Working with Suffering in Living and Dying* (Oxford: Oxford University Press, 2000).

Kidel, Mark and Susan Rowe-Leete, eds. *The Meaning of Illness* (London: Routledge Kegan & Paul, 1989).

Knudson, R.M. "Significant Dreams: Bizarre or Beautiful?" *Dreaming: Journal of the Association for the Study of Dreams* 11, no. 4 (2001).

—— and S. Minier. "The Ongoing Significance of Significant Dreams: The Case of the Bodiless Head," *Dreaming: Journal of the Association for the Study of Dreams* 9, no. 4 (1999).

Kugelmann, Robert. *The Windows of Soul: Psychological Physiology of the Human Eye and Primary Glaucoma* (Lewisburg, Penn.: Bucknell University Press, 1983).

Kugler, Paul K. "Image and Sound," *Spring: An Annual of Archetypal Psychology and Jungian Thought* (1978).

——. "The Phonetic Imagination," *Spring: An Annual of Archetypal Psychology and Jungian Thought* (1979).

——, and James Hillman. "The Autonomous Psyche," *Spring: An Annual of Archetypal Psychology and Jungian Thought* (1985).

——. "The Alchemical Theatre: Notes from the Pantheatre Laboratory at Malérargues," *Sphinx: A Journal for Archetypal Psychology and the Arts* 2 (1989).

——. "The Subject of Dreams," *Dreaming* 3, no. 2 (1993).

——, ed. *Jungian Perspectives on Clinical Supervision* (Einsiedeln: Daimon Verlag, 1995).

——. "Psychic Imagining: A Bridge Between Subject and Object," in *The Cambridge Companion to Jung*, ed. P. Young-Eisendrath and T. Dawson (below).

——. "Childhood Seduction: Material and Immaterial Facts," in *Fire in the Stone: The Alchemy of Desire*, ed. S. Marlan (below).

——. *The Alchemy of Discourse: Sound, Image, and Psyche* (Einsiedeln: Daimon Verlag, 2002).

——. "Psyche, Language and Biology: The Argument for a Co-Evolutionary Approach," in *Controversies in Analytical Psychology*, ed. R. Withers (New York: Brunner-Routledge, 2003).

Lambert, Kenneth. "Reflections on a Critique of Hillman's Approach to the Dream by W.A. Shelburne," *Journal of Analytical Psychology* 29, no. 1 (1984).

Landes, Donald A. and Azucena Cruz-Pierre, eds. *Exploring the Work of Edward S. Casey: Giving Voice to Place, Memory, and Imagination* (London: Bloomsbury, 2013).

Landry, Joseph. "Archetypal Psychology and the Twelve-Step Movement," *Spring: A Journal of Archetype and Culture* 58 (1995).

Lauter, Estella and Carol Schreier Rupprecht, eds. *Feminist Archetypal Theory: Interdisciplinary Re-Visions of Jungian Thought* (Knoxville: University of Tennessee Press, 1985).

Leveranz, John. "The Sacred Disease," *Dragonflies: Studies in Imaginal Psychology* 1, no. 2 (1979).

Loewe, Eva. *Sofferenza e bellezza* (Bergamo: Moretti & Vitali, 1998).

Lockhart, Russell A. "Cancer in Myth and Disease," *Spring: An Annual of Archetypal Psychology and Jungian Thought* (1977).

——. "Words as Eggs," *Dragonflies: Studies in Imaginal Psychology* 1, no. 1 (1978).

——. "Psyche in Hiding," *Quadrant: The Journal of Contemporary Jungian Thought* 13 (1980).

——. *Words as Eggs: Psyche in Language and Clinic* (Dallas: Spring Publications, 1983).

López-Pedraza, Rafael. "Responses and Contributions," *Spring: An Annual of Archetypal Psychology and Jungian Thought* (1971).

——. "Moon Madness – Titanic Love: A Meeting of Pathology and Poetry," in *Images of the Untouched*, ed. J. Stroud and G. Thomas (below).

——. *Anselm Kiefer: The Psychology of "After the Catastrophe"* (New York: George Braziller, 1996).

——. *Dionysus in Exile: On the Repression of the Body and Emotion* (Wilmette, Ill.: Chiron Publications, 2000).

——. *Hermes and His Children* (Einsiedeln: Daimon Verlag, 2010).

——. *Cultural Anxiety* (Einsiedeln: Daimon Verlag, 2012).

Lorenzi, Patrizia. "Nel segno della lontananza. La donna e il desiderio dell'altrove," in *Un oscuro impulso interiore*, ed. F. Donfrancesco (above).

Maclagan, David. "Methodical Madness," *Spring: An Annual of Archetypal Psychology and Jungian Thought* (1983).

——. "The Art of Madness and the Madness of Art," *Raw Vision* 27 (1999).

——. *Psychological Aesthetics: Painting, Feeling and Making Sense* (London and Philadelphia: Jessica Kingsley Publishers, 2001).

Mahdi, Louise Carus, Steven Foster, and Meredith Little, eds. *Betwixt and Between: Patterns of Masculine and Feminine Initiation* (La Salle, Ill.: Open Court, 1987).

Marlan, Stanton. "The Wandering Uterus: Dream and the Pathologized Image," in *Carl Jung and Soul Psychology*, ed. K. Gibson et. al. (above).

——, ed. *Salt and the Alchemical Soul: Three Essays* (Woodstock, Conn.: Spring Publications, 1995).

——. "Archetypal Psychology, Postmodernism and the Symbolic Function," *Methods: A Journal For Human Science* (1996).

——, ed. *Fire in the Stone: The Alchemy of Desire* (Wilmette, Ill.: Chiron Publications, 1997).

——. "The Metaphor of Light and its Deconstruction in Jung's Alchemical Vision," in *Jung and Phenomenology*, ed. R. Brooke (above).

——. "The Metaphor of Light and Renewal in Taoist Alchemy and Jungian Analysis," *Quadrant: The Journal of Contemporary Jungian Thought* 30, no. 2 (Summer 2001).

——, ed. *Archetypal Psychologies: Reflections in Honor of James Hillman* (New Orleans: Spring Journal Books, 2008).

May, Josephine and Martin Groder. "Jungian Thought and Dynamical Systems: A New Science of Archetypal Psychology," *Psychological Perspectives* 20, no. 1 (1989).

McConeghey, Howard. "Art Education and Archetypal Psychology," *Spring: An Annual of Archetypal Psychology and Jungian Thought* (1981).

——. *Art and Soul* (Woodstock, Conn.: Spring Publications, 2002).

McNeely, Deldon Anne. *Animus Aeternus: Exploring the Inner Masculine* (Toronto: Inner City Books, 1991).

——. *Mercury Rising: Women, Evil, and the Trickster Gods* (Woodstock, Conn.: Spring Publications, 1996).

——. "The Case of Joan: An Archetypal Approach," in *The Cambridge Companion to Jung*, ed. P. Young-Eisendrath and T. Dawson (below).

McNiff, Shaun. *Art as Medicine: Creating a Therapy of the Imagination* (Boston: Shambhala, 2012).

——. *Earth Angels: Engaging the Sacred in Everyday Things* (Boston: Shambhala, 1995).

——. *Art-Based Research* (London: Jessica Kingsley Publishers, 1998).

——. *Trust the Process: An Artist's Guide to Letting Go* (Boston: Shambhala, 1998).

——. *Art Heals: How Creativity Cures the Soul* (Boston: Shambhala, 2004).

Meade, Michael. *Men and the Water of Life: Initiation and the Tempering of Men* (San Francisco: Harper, 1993).

Micklem, Niel. "On Hysteria: The Mythical Syndrome," *Spring: An Annual of Archetypal Psychology and Jungian Thought* (1974).

——. "The Intolerable Image: The Mythic Background of Psychosis," *Spring: An Annual of Archetypal Psychology and Jungian Thought* (1979).

——. "Lightning Conduction and the Psychopathology of Convulsion," *Spring: An Annual of Archetypal Psychology and Jungian Thought* (1983).

——. *The Nature of Hysteria* (London and New York: Routledge, 1996).

Miller, David. L. "Polytheism and Archetypal Psychology," *Journal of the American Academy of Religion* 40 (1972).

——. "Fairy Tale or Myth," *Spring: An Annual of Archetypal Psychology and Jungian Thought* (1976).

——. "Images of Happy Ending," *Eranos Yearbook* 44 (1975).

——. "Imaginings No End," *Eranos Yearbook* 46 (1977).

——. *The New Polytheism* (Dallas: Spring Publications, 1981).

——. "Rhythms of Silenus in a Poetics of Christ," *Eranos Yearbook* 47 (1978).

——. "Between God and the Gods: Trinity," *Eranos Yearbook* 49 (1980).

——, ed. *Jung and the Interpretation of the Bible* (New York: Continuum, 1981).

——. "The Two Sandals of Christ: Descent into History and into Hell," *Eranos Yearbook* 50 (1981).

——. "The Holy Ghost and the Grateful Dead," *Eranos Yearbook* 52 (1983).

——. "Through a Looking Glass: The World as Enigma," *Eranos Yearbook* 55 (1986).

——. "Prometheus, St. Peter, and the Rock: Identity and Difference in Modern Literature," *Eranos Yearbook* 57 (1988).

——. "The Fire Is in the Mind," *Spring: A Journal of Archetype and Culture* 56 (1994).

——. "'A Myth Is As Good As a Smile!' The Mythology of a Consumerist Culture," in *Psychology at the Threshold*, ed. D.P. Slattery and L. Corbett (below).

——. *Hells and Holy Ghosts: A Theopoetics of Christian Belief* (New Orleans: Spring Journal Books, 2004).

——. *Three Faces of God: Traces of the Trinity in Literature and Life* (New Orleans: Spring Journal Books, 2005).

——. *Christs: Meditations on Archetypal Images in Christian Theology* (New Orleans: Spring Journal Books, 2005).

Mogenson, Greg. *A Most Accursed Religion: When A Trauma Becomes God* (Putnam, Conn.: Spring Publications, 2005).

——. *Greeting the Angels: An Imaginal View of the Mourning Process* (Amityville, N.Y.: Baywood Publishing, 1992).

——. "Children of Hell," *Spring: A Journal of Archetype and Culture* 55 (1994).

——. *The Dove in the Consulting Room: Hysteria and the Anima in Bollas and Jung* (London and New York: Brunner Routledge, 2003).

——. *Northern Gnosis: Thor, Baldr, and the Volsungs in the Thought of Freud and Jung* (New Orleans: Spring Journal Books, 2005).

Moore, Thomas. "Musical Therapy," *Spring: An Annual of Archetypal Psychology and Jungian Thought* (1978).

——. "Artemis and the Puer," in *Puer Papers*, ed. J. Hillman (Dallas: Spring Publications, 1979).

——. "Images in Asthma: Notes for a Study of Disease," *Dragonflies: Studies in Imaginal Psychology* 1 (1979).

——. "James Hillman: Psychology with Soul," *Religious Studies Review* 6 (1980).

——, ed. *A Blue Fire: Selected Writings of James Hillman* (New York: Harper & Row, 1989).

——. *The Planets Within: The Astrological Psychology of Marsilio Ficino* (Herndon, Virginia: Lindisfarne Press, 1990).

——. *Care of the Soul: A Guide for Cultivating Depth and Sacredness in Everyday Life* (New York: Harper Collins, 1992).

———. *Soul Mates: Honoring the Mystery of Love and Relationship* (New York: Harper Collins, 1994).

———. *The Soul of Sex: Cultivating Life as an Act of Love* (New York: Harper Collins, 1998).

———. *Dark Nights of the Soul: A Guide to Finding Your Way Through Life's Ordeals* (New York: Gotham Books, 2004).

———. *Dark Eros: The Imagination of Sadism* (Putnam, Conn.: Spring Publications, 2005).

———. *The Re-Enchantment of Everyday Life* (New York: Harper Collins, 1996).

———, ed. *The Education of the Heart: Readings and Sources for Care of the Soul, Soul Mates, and The Re-Enchantment of Everyday Life.* (New York: Harper Collins, 1996).

———. *Rituals of the Imagination* (Dallas: The Dallas Institute Publications, 2000).

Moscatello, Clara and Antonio Antonelli. "Da Heidegger a Hillman. Verso una psicoterapia come narrazione e come poiesis," *Psichiatria e psicoterapia analitica* 5 (1986).

Mottana, Paolo. *Miti d'oggi nell'educazione: E opportune contromisure* (Milan: Franco Angeli, 2000).

———. "La controeducazione di James Hillman," in *L'anima e il selvatico: Idee per "controeducare,"* ed. P. Mottana and N. Lucatelli (Bergamo: Moretti & Vitali, 2009).

Neack, L. and R.M. Knudson. "Re-Imagining the Sovereign State: Beginning an Interdisciplinary Dialogue," *Alternatives* 21 (1996).

Neville, Bernie. "The Myths We Teach By," *Australian Journal of Adult and Community Education* 32, no. 3 (November 1992).

———. "The Charm of Hermes: Hillman, Lyotard, and the Post-Modern Condition," *Journal of Analytical Psychology* (July 1992).

———. "The Polytheistic Classroom," *The International Journal of Transpersonal Studies* 12, no. 2 (1993).

———. "Addressing Planetary Pathology," *Psychotherapy in Australia* 6, no. 2 (1995).

———. "Seeing Through the Postmodern Organization," *Temenos* (Spring 1995).

———. "Dealing With Postmodern Pathology," *Futures* 26, no. 10 (December 1996).

———. "Prometheus, the Technologist," *The International Journal of Transpersonal Studies* 15, no. 2 (December 1996).

———. *Educating Psyche: Imagination, Emotion and the Unconscious in Learning* (Melbourne: David Lovell Publishing, 2012).

———. *The Life of Things: Therapy and the Soul of the World* (Ross on Wye: PCCS Books, 2012).

Newman, K.D. "Counter-Transference and Consciousness," *Spring: An Annual of Archetypal Psychology and Jungian Thought* (1980).

Nicholsen, Shierry Weber. *The Love of Nature and the End of the World: The Unspoken Dimensions of Environmental Concern* (Cambridge, Mass.: The MIT Press, 2002).

Noel, Daniel C. "Veiled Kabir: C.G. Jung's Phallic Self-Image," *Spring: An Annual of Archetypal Psychology and Jungian Thought* (1974).

——. *Approaching Earth: A Search for the Mythic Significance of the Space Age* (New York: Amity House, 1986).

——, ed. *Paths to the Power of Myth: Joseph Campbell and the Study of Religion* (New York: Crossroad, 1990).

——. *The Soul of Western Shamanism: Western Fantasies, Imaginal Realities* (New York: Continuum, 1998).

Odajnyk, V.W. "The Psychologist as Artist: The Imaginal World of James Hillman," *Quadrant: The Journal of Contemporary Jungian Thought* 17/1 (1984).

Ogilvy, James. *Many-Dimensional Man: Decentralizing Self, Society, and the Sacred* (New York: Oxford University Press, 1977).

Olivier, Richard. *Inspirational Leadership: Henry V and the Muse of Fire – Timeless Insights from Shakespeare's Greatest Leader* (London and Boston: Nicholas Braeley Publishing, 2013).

Ottmann, Klaus, ed. *Color Symbolism: The Eranos Lectures* (Putnam, Conn.: Spring Publications, 2005).

Pardo, Enrique. "Dis-membering Dionysus: Image and Theatre," *Spring: An Annual of Archetypal Psychology and Jungian Thought* (1984).

——. "The Theatres of Boredom and Depression: Two Gateways to Imagination," *Spring: An Annual of Archetypal Psychology and Jungian Thought* (1988).

——. "Archetypal Riddles/Baroque Solutions," *Sphinx: A Journal for Archetypal Psychology and the Arts* 1 (1988).

——. "Pan's 'Theatre of the World': Notes on 'Object-Metaphore,'" *Spring: An Annual of Archetypal Psychology and Jungian Thought* 49 (1989).

——. "Dionysos: A Tragic Putrefactio and a Baroque Solution," *Sphinx: A Journal for Archetypal Psychology and the Arts* 2 (1989).

——. "Inspiration, Eros and Error: Failure in 'The Alchemical Theatre,'" *Sphinx: A Journal for Archetypal Psychology and the Arts* 3 (1990).

——. "The Angel's Hideout: Between Dance and Theatre," *Performance Research* 3, no. 2 (1998).

Paris, Ginette. "Theater and Therapy: Dionysos in Everyday Life," *Sphinx: A Journal for Archetypal Psychology and the Arts* 2 (1989).

——. "If You Invite the Gods to Your Marriage," *Spring: A Journal of Archetype and Culture* 60 (1996).

——. "Broken Promises – Psychotherapy at the End of the Twentieth Century," *Sphinx: A Journal for Archetypal Psychology and the Arts* 7 (1996).

——. "Everyday Epiphanies," in *On the Sublime in Psychoanalysis, Archetypal Psychology, and Psychotherapy*, ed. P. Clarkson (above).

——. "Broken Promises," *Spring: A Journal of Archetype and Culture* 64 (1998).

——. "A Conversation between Ginette Paris and James Hillman on Ecology," *The Salt Journal* 1 (June/July 1998).

——. "Ginette Paris interviews James Hillman on Rituals," *The Salt Journal* 1 (April/May 1998).

——. "Mythology of Marriage," in *Psychology at the Threshold*, ed. D.P. Slattery and L. Corbett (below).

——. "Hillman-Giegerich: What Is Going On?" Keynote address, International Symposium of Archetypal Psychology, University of California at Santa Barbara, August – September 2000, in *Depth Psychology*, ed. D.P. Slattery and L. Corbett (below).

——. *Pagan Meditations: The Worlds of Aphrodite, Artemis, and Hestia*, trans. G. Moore (Putnam: Spring Publications, 2005).

——. *Pagan Grace: Dionysos, Hermes, and Goddess Memory in Daily Life*, trans. J. Mott (Putnam, Conn.: Spring Publications, 2005).

——. *The Psychology of Abortion* (formerly *The Sacrament of Abortion*), trans. J. Mott (Putnam, Conn.: Spring Publications, 2007).

——. *Wisdom of the Psyche: Depth Psychology after Neuroscience* (New York: Routledge, 2007).

——. *Heartbreak: New Approaches to Healing – Recovering from Lost Love and Mourning* (Minneapolis: Mill City Press, 2011).

Parkes, Graham. *Composing the Soul: Reaches of Nietzsche's Psychology* (Chicago: University of Chicago Press, 1994).

Perez, Luciano. "Aspetti demonici del Sé," *Anima* (1998).

——. "L'espressione dei sentimenti," *I quaderni di Yseos* (1999).

——. "Il giardino dell'alchimia o la clinica sognata," in *I territori dell'alchimia*, ed. R. Ortoleva and F. Testa (Bergamo: Moretti & Vitali, 1999).

——. "L'ombra e il sacro," *I quaderni di Yseos* (2000).

——. "Geografie e topografie reali, immaginarie e immaginali," *I quaderni di Yseos* (2001).

Perlman, Michael. *Imaginal Memory and the Place of Hiroshima* (Albany, N.Y.: State University of New York Press, 1988).

——. *The Power of Trees: The Reforesting of the Soul* (Dallas: Spring Publications, 1994).

——. *Hiroshima Forever: The Ecology of Mourning* (Barrytown, N.Y.: Station Hill Arts, 1995).

Poncé, Charles. *Papers Towards a Radical Metaphysics: Alchemy* (Berkeley: North Atlantic Books, 1983).

——. *Working the Soul: Reflections on Jungian Psychology* (Berkeley: North Atlantic Books, 1988).

——. *The Archetype of the Unconscious and the Transfiguration of Therapy: Reflections on Jungian Psychology* (Berkeley: North Atlantic Books, 1993).

Popović, Velimir B. "Archetypal Psychology," *Delo* XXXIV (1988).

——. "Ascetic Body – Lustful Soul: An Archetypal Approach to the Psychology of Anorexia Nervosa," *Harvest* 57 (1991).

——. "Psyche, Mythos and Pathos," in *Etnopsihologija danas* (Ethnopsychology Today), ed. B. Jovanović (Beograd: Treći milenijum, 1992).

——. "Why Imaginal Pathology?" in *Antropologija bolesti i zdravlja* (Anthropology of Illness and Health), ed. M. Djurić-Srejić and Č. Hadžinikolić (Belgrade: Serbian Anthropological Society, 2000).

Quintaes, Marcus. "O dia em que Caetano convidou um homem a subir ao palco: Reflexões em Psicologia Arquetípica," in *O masculino em questão*, ed. W. Boechat (Rio de Janeiro: Editora Vozes, 1997).

——. Various online articles at *www.rubedo.psc.br/inicio.htm.*

Richards, Stanley. *The Golden Apples of Venus: Essays in Archetypal Psychology* (Christchurch: Association for Analytical Psychology, 1996).

——. *Many Places of the Soul: An Introduction to Archetypal Psychology* (Christchurch: Association for Analytical Psychology, 1998).

Romanyshyn, Robert. "Psychological Language and the Voice of Things," *Dragonflies: Studies in Imaginal Psychology* 1, no. 2 (1979).

——. "Looking at the Light: Reflections of the Mutable Body," *Dragonflies: Studies in Imaginal Psychology* 2, no. 1 (1980).

——. *Psychological Life: From Science to Metaphor* (Austin: University of Texas Press, 1982).

——. "Depression and the American Dream: The Struggle with Home," in *Pathologies of the Modern Self: Postmodern Studies on Narcissism, Schizophrenia, and Depression*, ed. D.M. Kleinberg-Levin (New York: New York University Press, 1987).

——. "Mirroring as Metaphor of Psychological Life," in *Self and Identity: Psychosocial Perspectives*, ed. K.M. Yardley and T.M. Honess (New York: John Wiley, 1987).

——. *Technology as Symptom and Dream* (London and New York: Routledge, 1989).

——. "Technology and Homecoming: Wilderness as Landscape of Soul," in *Jung in the Context of Southern Africa*, ed. G.S. Saayman (Boston: Sigo Press, 1990).

——. "Starry Nights, Sexual Love and the Rhythms of the Soul," *Sphinx: A Journal for Archetypal Psychology and the Arts* 7 (1996).

——. "Egos, Angels and the Colors of Nature," *Alexandria* 4 (1997).

——. *The Soul In Grief: Love, Death, and Transformation* (Berkeley: North Atlantic Press, 1999).

——. *Mirror and Metaphor: Images and Stories of Psychological Life* (Pittsburgh: Trivium Publications, 2001).

——. *Ways of the Heart: Essays Toward an Imaginal Psychology* (Pittsburgh: Trivium Publications, 2002).

Rossi, Ernest Lawrence. "Perspectives: The New Archetypal Psychology," *Psychological Perspectives* 18, no. 2 (1987).

Rupprecht, Carol Schreier. "Archetypal Theory and Criticism," in *The Johns Hopkins Guide to Literary Theory & Criticism*, ed. M. Groden, M. Kreiswirth, and I. Szeman (Baltimore: The Johns Hopkins University Press, 2005).

Rylance, Mark. *I Am Shakespeare* (London: Nick Hern Books, 2012).

Sacco, Daniela. "Le trame intrecciate di Mnemosyne: Jung, Warburg e Hillman in dialogo," in *Un remoto presente*, ed. F. Donfrancesco (Bergamo: Moretti & Vitali, 2002).

Samuels, Andrew. *Jung and the Post-Jungians* (London and New York: Routledge, 1999).

——. "Response to James Hillman's 'Yellowing of the Work,'" in *Proceedings of the 11th International Congress for Analytical Psychology, Paris 1989*, ed. M.A. Mattoon (Einsiedeln: Daimon Verlag, 1989).

Sardello, Robert J. "Hermeneutical Reading: An Approach to the Classic Texts of Psychology," in *Duquesne Studies in Phenomenological Psychology*, vol. II, ed. A. Giorgi, C.T. Fischer, and E.L. Murray (Pittsburgh: Duquesne University Press, 1975).

——. "Ensouling Language," *Dragonflies: Studies in Imaginal Psychology* 1, no. 1 (1978).

——. "An Empirical-Phenomenological Study of Fantasy," *Psychocultural Review* 2 (1978).

——. *Educating with Soul*. Pamphlet, Center for Civic Leadership, University of Dallas, 1979.

——. "Beauty and Violence: The Play of Imagination in the World," *Dragonflies: Studies in Imaginal Psychology* 2, no. 1 (1980).

——. "On Seeing Through the World," *Spring: An Annual of Archetypal Psychology and Jungian Thought* (1983).

——. and Randolph Severson, eds. *Money and the Soul of the World* (Dallas: The Pegasus Foundation, 1983).

——. "Taking the Side of Things: Notes on Psychological Activism," *Spring: An Annual of Archetypal Psychology and Jungian Thought* (1984).

——. "Saving the Things or How to Avoid the Bomb," *Spring: An Annual of Archetypal Psychology and Jungian Thought* (1985).

——. and Gail Thomas, eds. *Stirrings of Culture: Essays from The Dallas Institute* (Dallas: The Dallas Institute Publications, 1986).

——, ed. *The Angels* (Dallas: The Dallas Institute Publications, 1994).

——. *Freeing the Soul from Fear* (New York: Riverhead Books, 2001).

——. *Facing the World with Soul: The Reimagination of Modern Life* (Hudson, N.Y.: Lindisfarne Press, 2004).

——. *Love and the Soul: Creating a Future for Earth* (Benson, North Carolina, and Berkeley: Goldenstone Press and North Atlantic Books, 2008).

——. *Silence: The Mystery of Wholeness* (Benson, North Carolina, and Berkeley: Goldenstone Press and North Atlantic Books, 2008).

——. *The Power of Soul: Living the Twelve Virtues* (Benson, North Carolina: Goldenstone Press, 2012).

Schenk, Ronald. *The Soul of Beauty: A Psychological Investigation of Appearance* (Lewisburg, Penn.: Bucknell University Press, 1992).

——. *Dark Light: The Appearance of Death in Everyday Life* (Albany, N.Y.: State University of New York Press, 2001).

——. *The Sunken Quest, the Wasted Fisher, the Pregnant Fish: Postmodern Reflections on Depth Psychology* (Wilmette, Ill.: Chiron Press, 2001).

Schwartz-Salant, Nathan, and Murray Stein, eds. *Gender and Soul in Psychotherapy* (Wilmette, Ill.: Chiron Press, 1992).

——, eds. *Archetypal Processes in Psychotherapy* (Wilmette, Ill.: Chiron Press, 1987).

Scott, Charles E. "On Hillman and Calvin," *Soundings* 63 (1980).

Sells, Benjamin. *The Soul of the Law* (Rockport, Mass.: Element, 1994).

——. *Order in the Court: Crafting a More Just World in Lawless Times* (Boston: Element, 1999).

——, ed. *Working with Images: The Theoretical Base of Archetypal Psychology* (Woodstock, Conn.: Spring Publications, 2000).

Severson, Randolph. "Titans Under Glass: A Recipe for the Recovery of Psychological Jargon," *Dragonflies: Studies in Imaginal Psychology* 1, no. 1 (1978).

——. "Puer's Wounded Wing: Reflections on the Psychology of Skin Disease," in *Puer Papers*, ed. J. Hillman (Dallas: Spring Publications, 1979).

Shelburne, W.A. "A Critique of James Hillman's Approach to the Dream," *Journal of Analytical Psychology* 29, no. 1 (1984).

Shunk, Gary and Virginia Taylor. "Conference: Character, Fate and Destiny – Authentic Threads in Life," *Round Table Review* 4, no. 3 (1997).

Simmer, Stephen. "The Academy of the Dead: On Boredom, Writer's Block, Footnotes and Deadlines," *Spring: An Annual of Archetypal Psychology and Jungian Thought* (1981).

Sipiora, Michael P. "A Soul's Journey: Camus, Tuberculosis, and Aphrodite," *Spring: An Annual of Archetypal Psychology and Jungian Thought* (1981).

——. "The Anima Mundi and the Fourfold: Hillman and Heidegger on the 'Idea' of the World," in *Pathways into the Jungian World*, ed. R. Brooke (above).

Slattery, Dennis Patrick. "Pan, Myth and Fantasy in Dostoevsky's *The Idiot*," *Canadian-American Slavic Studies* 17, no. 3 (Fall 1983).

——. *The Idiot: Dostoevsky's Fantastic Prince* (New York: Peter Lang Publishing, 1983).

——. "Seized by the Muse: Dostoevsky's Convulsive Poetics in *The Idiot*," *Literature and Medicine Issue: Writers With Chronic Illness* 18, no. 1 (1999).

——. *The Wounded Body: Remembering the Markings of Flesh* (Albany, N.Y.: State University of New York Press, 1999).

——. "The Narrative Play of Memory in Epic," in *The Epic Cosmos*, ed. L. Allums (Dallas: The Dallas Institute Publications, 2000).

—— and Lionel Corbett, eds. *Psychology at the Threshold: Selected Papers from the Proceedings of the International Conference at University of California, Santa Barbara, 2000* (Carpinteria: Pacifica Graduate Institute Publications, 2000).

——. *Depth Psychology: Meditations in the Field* (Einsiedeln: Daimon Verlag, 2004).

Smith, Evans Lansing. *Ricorso and Revelation: An Archetypal Poetics of Modernism* (Columbia, South Carolina: Camden House, 1995).

Stamper, Mary. "Can Therapy be an Addiction?" *Round Table Review* 3, no. 3 (1996).

Stein, Murray. "The Devouring Father," in *Fathers and Mothers*, ed. P. Berry (above).

——. "Hephaistos: A Pattern of Introversion," *Spring: An Annual of Archetypal Psychology and Jungian Thought* (1973).

——. "On Narcissus," *Spring: An Annual of Archetypal Psychology and Jungian Thought* (1976).

——. "Hera: Bound and Unbound," *Spring: An Annual of Archetypal Psychology and Jungian Thought* (1977).

——. "On Jealousy," *Psychological Perspectives* (1978).

—— and John Hollwitz, eds. *Psyche and Sports: Baseball, Hockey, Martial Arts, Running, Tennis* (Wilmette, Ill.: Chiron Publications, 1994).

——. *In Midlife* (Putnam, Conn.: Spring Publications, 2004).

Stein, Robert. "Body and Psyche: An Archetypal View of Psychosomatic Phenomena," *Spring: An Annual of Archetypal Psychology and Jungian Thought* (1976).

——. "Coupling/Uncoupling: Reflections of the Evolution of the Marriage Archetype," *Spring: An Annual of Archetypal Psychology and Jungian Thought* (1981).

——. *The Betrayal of the Soul in Psychotherapy* (Formerly *Incest and Human Love*) (Woodstock, Conn.: Spring Journal Books, 1998).

Stevens, Anthony. *Ariadne's Clue: A Guide to the Symbols of Humankind* (Princeton, N.J.: Princeton University Press, 2001).

Stoknes, Per Espen. "Intervju med James Hillman: Hvalfangst, teknologi og psykologisk aktivisme," *Impuls: Tidsskrift for Psykologi* 47, no. 2 (1993).

——. "Arketypisk Natur – Hillman og Stoknes, to økopsykologer i samtale," *Flux* 11 (1995).

——. *Sjelens Landskap: Refleksjoner over Natur og Myter* (Oslo: J.W. Cappelens Forlag, 1996).

Stroppa, Carla. "La credenza dimenticata," in *Il ricordo del presente: Memoria e formazione del senso* (Bergamo: Moretti & Vitali, 2001).

——. "Verso la forma," in *I territori dell'alchimia: Jung e oltre*, ed. R. Ortoleva and F. Testa (Bergamo: Moretti & Vitali, 1999).

——. "Sentieri della nostalgia," *Anima* (1999).

——. (2001). "Così vicino così lontano. Scrittura e psicoanalisi," in *Per nascosti sentieri*, ed. F. Donfrancesco (above).

Stroud, Joanne H. *The Bonding of Will and Desire* (New York: Continuum, 1994).

——, ed. *The Olympians: Ancient Deities as Archetypes* (Dallas: The Dallas Institute Publications, 1995).

—— and Gail Thomas, eds. *Images of the Untouched: Virginity in Psyche, Myth, and Community* (Dallas: The Dallas Institute Publications, 1982).

Solié, Pierre. *Psychanalyse et Imaginal* (Paris: Imago, 1980).

Sugg, Richard P. *Jungian Literary Criticism* (Evanston, Ill.: Northwestern University Press, 1992).

Tacey, David. "Twisting and Turning with James Hillman," in *Post-Jungians Today*, ed. A. Casement (above).

——. *Jung and the New Age* (New York: Brunner-Routledge, 2002).

Tatham, Peter. *The Makings of Maleness: Men, Women, and the Flight of Daedalus* (New York: New York University Press, 1992).

Te Paske, Bradley A. *Rape and Ritual: A Psychological Study* (Toronto: Inner City Books, 1982).

Thomas, Gail, ed. *The City as Dwelling: Walking, Sitting, Shaping* (Dallas: The Dallas Institute Publications, 1983).

——, ed. *Pegasus: The Spirit of Cities* (Dallas: The Dallas Institute Publications, 1993).

——, ed. *The Muses* (Dallas: The Dallas Institute Publications, 1994).

Tibaldi, Marta. "In forma narrativa. La scrittura autobiografica dell'anima," in *Un oscuro impulso interiore*, ed. F. Donfrancesco (above).

——. "La passione narrativa. Appunti per una cura immaginale," in *Per nascosti sentieri*, ed. F. Donfrancesco (above).

Vedfelt, Ole. *The Dimensions of Dreams: The Nature, Function and Interpretation of Dreams* (London and Philadelphia: Jessica Kingsley Publishers, 2002).

Vitale, Augusto. "Saturn: The Transformation of the Father," in *Fathers and Mothers*, ed. P. Berry (above).

De Voogd, Stephanie. "C.G. Jung: Psychologist of the Future, 'Philosopher' of the Past," *Spring: An Annual of Archetypal Psychology and Jungian Thought* (1977).

——. "Fantasy vs. Fiction: Jung's Kantianism Appraised," in *Jung in Modern Perspective*, ed. R.K. Papadopoulous, G.S. Saayman (Hounslow, England: Wildwood House, 1984).

Vogt, Gregory Max. *Return to Father: Archetypal Dimensions of the Patriarch* (Dallas: Spring Publications, 1991).

Walker, Steven F. *Jung and the Jungians on Myth: An Introduction* (London and New York: Routledge, 2002).

Wallace, James A. *Imaginal Preaching: An Archetypal Perspective* (Mahwah, N.J.: Paulist Press, 1995).

Watkins, Mary M. "Six Approaches to the Image in Art Therapy," *Spring: An Annual of Archetypal Psychology and Jungian Thought* (1981).

——. "In Dreams Begin Responsibilities: Moral Imagination and Peace Action," in *Facing Apocalypse*, ed. V. Andrews et al. (above).

——. "Mother and Child: Some Teachings of Desire," in *Fathers and Mothers*, ed. P. Berry (above).

——. "From Individualism to the Interdependent Self: Changing Paradigms in Psychotherapy," *Psychological Perspectives* 27 (1992).

——. "Depth Psychology and the Liberation of Being," in *Jung and Phenomenology*, ed. R. Brooke (above).

——. "Seeding Liberation: A Dialogue Between Depth Psychology and Liberation Psychology," in *Depth Psychology: Meditations in the Field*, ed. D.P. Slattery and L. Corbett (above).

——. and Helene Shulman Lorenz. "Silenced Knowings, Forgotten Springs: Paths to Healing in the Wake of Colonialism" (published online at *www.mythinglinks.org/LorenzWatkins.html*).

——. *Waking Dreams* (Woodstock, Conn.: Spring Publications, 1998).

—— and Helene Shulman Lorenz. "Individuation, Seeing-through, and Liberation: Depth Psychology and Culture," *Quadrant* (2003).

——. *Invisible Guests: The Development of Imaginal Dialogues* (Putnam, Conn.: Spring Publications, 2005).

—— and Helene Shulman. *Toward Psychologies of Liberation* (New York: Palgrave Macmillan, 2008).

Whan, Michael. "'Don Juan,' Trickster, and Hermeneutic Understanding," *Spring: An Annual of Archetypal Psychology and Jungian Thought* (1978).

——. "Hermetic Silence and Psychotherapy," *Harvest: Journal for Jungian Studies* 26 (1980).

——. "On the Nature of Practice," *Spring: An Annual of Archetypal Psychology and Jungian Thought* (1987).

———. "Chiron's Wound: Some Reflections on the Wounded-Healer," in *Archetypal Processes in Psychotherapy*, ed. N. Schwartz-Salant and M. Stein (above).

———. "Self-Knowledge, Ethos and Depth Psychology," *Harvest: Journal for Jungian Studies* 33 (1987–88).

———. "Archaic Mind and Modernist Consciousness," *Spring: A Journal of Archetype and Culture* 56 (1994).

———. "Registering Psychotherapy as an Institutional Neurosis: or, Compounding the Estrangement Between Soul and World," *European Journal of Psychotherapy, Counseling and Health* 2, no. 3 (1999).

Winquist, Charles. "The Epistemology of Darkness," *Journal of the American Academy of Religion* 49 (1981).

Young-Eisendrath, Polly and Terence Dawson, eds. *The Cambridge Companion to Jung* (Cambridge: Cambridge University Press, 2008).

Zabriskie, Beverley D. "Exiles and Orphans: Jung, Paracelsus, and the Healing Images of Alchemy," *Quadrant* 26 no. 1–2 (1995).

———. "*Fermentation* in Jung's Alchemy," in *Zürich 95: Open Questions in Analytical Psychology (Proceedings of the Thirteenth International Congress for Analytical Psychology)*, ed. M.A. Mattoon (Einsiedeln: Daimon Verlag, 1997).

———. "The One and Many Souls of New York City," in *Psyche and the City: A Soul's Guide to the Modern Metropolis*, ed. T. Singer (New Orleans: Spring Journal Books, 2012).

Ziegler, Alfred J. "Rousseauian Optimism, Natural Distress and Dream Research," *Spring: An Annual of Archetypal Psychology and Jungian Thought* (1976).

———. "Rheumatics and Stoics," *Spring: An Annual of Archetypal Psychology and Jungian Thought* (1979).

———. *Archetypal Medicine*, trans. G.V. Hartman, W. Barscht, and C. Landry (Dallas: Spring Publications, 1980).

———. "On Pain and Punishment," *Spring: An Annual of Archetypal Psychology and Jungian Thought* (1982).

———. *Wirklichkeitswahn: Die Menschheit auf der Flucht von sich selbst* (Zurich: Schweizer Spiegel Verlag, 1983).

———. *Bilder einer Schattenmedizin* (Zurich: Schweizer Spiegel Verlag, 1987).

———. "Morbistic Rituals," in *The Meaning of Illness*, ed. M. Kidel and S. Rowe-Leete (London: Routledge Kegan & Paul, 1989).

———. "Illness as Descent into the Body," in *Meeting the Shadow*, ed. C. Zweig and J. Abrams (below).

Zoja, Luigi. *Nascere non basta: Iniziazione e tossicodipendenza* (Milano: Raffaello Cortina, 1985).

——. *Growth and Guilt: Psychology and the Limits of Development* (London and New York: Routledge, 1995).

——. "Analysis and Tragedy," in *Post-Jungians Today*, ed. A. Casement (above).

——. *Coltivare l'anima* (Bergamo: Moretti & Vitali, 1999).

——. *Drugs, Addiction and Initiation: The Modern Search for Ritual* (Einsiedeln: Daimon Verlag, 2012).

——. *Il gesto di Ettore. Preistoria, storia e scomparsa del padre* (Turin: Bollati Boringhieri, 2003).

——. "L'anima senza tragedia nel secolo dell'analisi," in *Per nascosti sentieri*, ed. F. Donfrancesco (above).

——. *The Father: Historical, Psychological and Cultural Perspectives*, trans. H. Martin (Philadelphia: Taylor & Francis, 2001).

—— and D. Williams, eds. *Jungian Reflections on September 11: A Global Nightmare* (Einsiedeln: Daimon Verlag, 2012).

Zweig, Connie, and Jeremiah Abrams, eds. *Meeting the Shadow: The Hidden Power of the Dark Side of Human Nature* (New York: Jeremy P. Tarcher/ Putnam, 1991).

—— and Steven Wolf. *Romancing the Shadow: A Guide to Soul Work for a Vital, Authentic Life* (New York: Ballantine Books, 1999).

C. Films, Plays, Performances and Festivals

Archetypal psychology has been of particular interest to artists in many media. Below is a small selection.

Conners, Nadia, and Leila Conners Petersen. *The 11th Hour*, 95 min. (2007)
The film explores our impact on the earth's ecosystems, featuring dialogues of experts from all over the world, including James Hillman.

Hunt, Helen. *Then She Found Me*, 100 min. (2007)
Hunt's directorial debut, based on a novel by Elinor Lipman. Hunt said it was Hillman's essay on betrayal that suddenly made everything click.

Jarman, Derek. *Caravaggio*, 93 min. (1986)
"In the retrospective of his work at the Barbican, there was a glass cabinet with the books Derek most admired and read. *The Myth of Analysis* was one of them. There are lines of dialogue in the script of his movie *Caravaggio* which are taken verbatim straight from Hillman. I don't think too many people know this." (Mark Kidel)

——. *Blue*, 79 min. (1993)
A narration of Jarman's experiences with AIDS and his vision as an artist shot against a plain, unchanging blue screen.

Kidel, Mark. *New York: The Secret African City,* 60 min. (1989)
  Yale professor Robert Farris Thompson discusses black religion and
  culture in New York.
——. *Derek Jarman: A Portrait,* 60 min. (1991)
  Portrait of Jarman's life and work as a painter, writer, and filmmaker.
——. *The Heart Has Reasons,* 52 min. (1993)
  An essay about heart disease and the symbolism of the heart. With
  contributions from James Hillman and Ginette Paris.
——. *The Architecture of the Imagination,* 150 min. (1994)
  A series of five 30-minute films about the symbolism of doors, windows,
  staircases, bridges, and towers. With James Hillman.
——. *Kind of Blue,* 52 min. (1994)
  An essay on melancholia. With James Hillman.

Meredith Monk. *impermanence* (ECM, 2008)
  Monk's "last song" uses words from Hillman's *A Force of Character.*

Olivier, Richard, et. al.
  Olivier Mythodrama, London
  (*http://www.oliviermythodrama.com*).

Pardo, Enrique, Linda Wise, and Liza Mayer.
  Panthéâtre, Paris and Malérargues
  (*http://www.pantheatre.com*).

Part Three

Why "Archetypal Psychology"?

Jungian, analytical, and complex are the three generally used terms for the psychology represented in this publication during the past thirty years. The subtitle of the 1970 issue of *Spring* ("An Annual of Archetypal Psychology and Jungian Thought") introduces a fourth: *archetypal*. Quite likely there are contrasts in these terms that are more than accents, and it seems worthwhile to characterize some of these differences.

The eponym Jungian is more than a common adjective; it evokes the emotional attachment to a man, to a history, to a body of thought and, especially, experience. Some who speak of themselves as "Jungians" had personal experience with Jung; nearly all have had experience of Jungian analysis. Because "Jung" continues to play a numinous role in the ideas, dreams, and fantasies of Jungians, the term musters psychic energy as an intimate symbol, stirring vital beliefs and feelings of loyalty. The name touches upon what Grinnell discusses as "psychological faith" and "personality."[1]

Since the appearance of "Jung" is unique to each person, this designation is intensely subjective. What makes a Jungian? Is "being a Jungian" truly a kind of being, that is, a way of existing in accordance with certain beliefs (even if unformulated) and practices (even if uncodified)? Or, have we become Jungians through association in a community of interests, through professional qualifications, or through tracing psychological lineage back to Jung by means of an analytical family tree? This last question raises further ones, since many feel themselves sympathetic to "the Jungian thing" and take part in it, and yet they have never been analyzed. Moreover, strictly speaking, Jungian derives from a family name and belongs to an actual family rather than to a following.

By meaning many things to many people, Jungian, like any symbol, provides an emotional atmosphere. But, just because of the emotions the word conjures, Jungian also constellates *kinship libido* with attendant passions of family feeling, sometimes called transference, sometimes called sibling rivalry, trailing Eros and Eris along. This shows in the exogamous hostility between the Jungian community and its ideas and "non-Jungians," and it shows within the Jungian community itself. Whitmont[2] and Guggenbühl[3] have each reflected upon aggression and destruction in relatively closed situations. The aggression and destruction released by Jungians against Jungians in the name of Jungian psychology may not be resolved merely through shifting terms, but it might be ameliorated by reflecting upon this familiar designation and what it can imply. These thorny issues have led us to use *Jungiana* to refer to the actual person of C.G. Jung, and *Jungian Thought* in tribute to a tradition that is difficult to describe otherwise.

The difference between complex and analytical was made clear in 1935 by Toni Wolff:[4]

> Recently Jung uses the term "complex psychology" mostly when he speaks of the whole area of his psychology particularly from the *theoretical* point of view. On the other hand, the description "analytical psychology" is appropriate when one is talking about the practice of psychological analysis.

As the name indicates, complex psychology builds upon the complex for its theory. This basis is empirical because it takes up the complex mainly through the association experiment, where measurements play the major role. Perhaps, because of this empirical origin, complex psychology inclines towards models from the natural sciences and their fantasies of objectivity. The association experiment is that part of Jung's work which can best be measured and demonstrated publicly. It is independent of therapy, an objective method that can be used with anybody. Upon it a theory of the psyche can be presented that attempts general validity and does not need the witnessing material of analytical cases. Individuals and their psychic material provide data for collections with which to advance psychology in general rather than the psyche of a specific analytical case. However, when theory follows scientific models, there are corresponding methods: statistics, questionnaires, measurements and machines for the study of dreams, types, psychosomatics, psychopharmaceutics, and synchronicity. The patient now may become an empirical subject and the clinic a laboratory setting in the interests of objective research into the general laws of complex behavior. A hope of complex psychology is to establish Jung's hypotheses, objectively and among a wider audience of the scientific and academic world beyond the one limited to Jungians or by analysis.

One could still use the description "complex" psychology, conceiving theory not on the models of science but in regard to the archetypal core of the complexes. Then we would be engaged more with symbolic thinking, and then psychological theory might better reflect both Jung's concerns with the metaphysical and imaginal and the soul. Nevertheless, the designation has one great disadvantage: it evokes Jung's first idea of the complex as a *disturbance* of consciousness. Despite all that he wrote afterwards concerning its value in all psychic life, the word retains pathological connotations – power complex, Oedipus complex, mother complex.

In 1896, Freud[5] first joined the word analysis to psyche in his new term "psychoanalytic" for describing a new method of therapy. Jung commented upon the naming of the new psychology in 1912:

> One could describe the psychology invented by [Freud] as "analytical psychology." Bleuler suggested the name "depth psychology," in order to indicate that Freudian psychology was concerned with the deeper regions or hinterland of the psyche, also called the unconscious. Freud himself was content just to name his method of investigation: he called it psychoanalysis.[6]

In 1929, Jung wrote:

> I prefer to call my own approach "analytical psychology" by which I mean something like a general concept embracing both psychoanalysis and individual psychology [Alfred Adler] as well as other endeavors in the field of "complex psychology."[7]

In following paragraphs Jung says that "analytical" is the word he uses for all the different psychological attempts "to solve the problem of the psyche." Clearly, analytical refers to the practice of therapy as problem-solving, to analysis as the work of making-conscious. When "analytical" defines our field, we are mainly occupied with what used to be called "the practical intellect." Several consequences flow from this.

With the practical in the foreground, analytical psychology is naturally interested in therapy and in the many questions of profession. It will also be searching for improved methods for problem-solving.

New directions are mainly practical: therapeutic techniques, groups, clinics provide fantasies for new ways to solve the problem of the psyche. There is also an obsessive focus upon analysis itself, especially the transference. Then, too, analytical psychology has interests naturally aligned with pastoral psychology and the "cure of souls," another path of problem-solving.

Unlike Freud's earliest use of the term, analysis today is more than a method. We are as well a profession, a mentality that analyzes (people, their "material," their "relationships"), and we have a big stake in a system: analysts, analysands, and an unconscious to be made conscious. Indeed, we can hardly get along without the unconscious. What is by definition a hypothesis has reified into a hypostasis filled with "real," "hard," and "tough" problems to be analyzed. If the unconscious calls for analysis, analytical psychology necessitates an unconscious.

In analytical psychology, the analyst is the psychologist and our psychology consists mainly in insights gained through analysis. This tends to limit our horizon. The idea of amplification may show what I mean. Even when analytical psychology extends into wide areas, study is for the context of therapy. We feel that amplification must be brought down to actual cases, else it becomes speculative fantasy. For analysts, the problem of the psyche is "located" in the soul of the individual and his situation as a case.

Jungian, analytical, and complex were never happy choices nor were they adequate to the psychology they tried to designate. It seems right to turn to a word that does reflect the characteristic approach of Jung, both to theory and to what actually goes on in practice, and to life in general. To call this psychology today *archetypal* follows from its historical development. The earlier terms have, in a sense, been superseded by the concept of the archetype, which Jung had not yet worked out when he named his psychology. The archetype is the most ontologically fundamental of all Jung's psychological concepts, with the advantage of precision and yet by definition partly indefinable and open. Psychic life rests upon these organs; even the self is conceptually subsumed among the archetypes; and they are the operative agents in Jung's idea of therapy. This designation reflects the deepened theory of Jung's later work, which attempts to solve psychological problems at a step beyond scientific models and therapy in the usual sense, because the soul's problems are no longer problems in the usual sense. Instead, one looks for the archetypal fantasies within the "models," the "objectivity," and the "problems." Already in 1912, Jung placed analysis within an archetypal frame, thereby freeing the archetypal from confinement to the analytical. Analysis may be an instrument for realizing the archetypes but it cannot embrace them. Placing archetypal prior to analytical gives the psyche a chance to move out of the consulting room. It gives an archetypal perspective to the consulting room itself. After all, analysis too is an enactment of an archetypal fantasy.

According to Jung,[8] myth best represents the archetypes. But myth proceeds from a realm that cannot legitimately be considered altogether human. Like the mythical, the archetypal transcends the human psyche, which implies the psyche's organs do not altogether belong to it. A true depth psychology is obliged by the nature of the psyche to go below or beyond the psyche. This fortunately offers a way out of the impasse of psychologizing, which has hindered the collaboration of some who too take their perspective from the archetypes but do not allow their location *in* the psyche. But we do not have to take the archetypes as primarily *psychic* structures; the psyche is only one place where they manifest. By psychologizing I also mean the tendency to attribute too much to the human and the psychic, burdening our lives with an over-weening sense of responsibility for matters that are not ours, but are archetypal, i.e., historical, mythical, psychoid – or instinctual in the sense of Robert Stein.[9]

Insights for this approach call for an archetypal eye that is difficult to acquire through focus upon persons and cases. This eye needs training through profound appreciation of history and biography, of the arts, of ideas and culture. Here, amplification becomes a valid way of doing psychology, necessary and sufficient in itself. Amplification can be a method of soul-making by finding the cultural in the psyche and thereby giving culture to the soul. A great deal can be done for the psyche and its healing, indirectly, through archetypal elucidation of its problems.

The mythical perspective may get us around another kind of psychologizing: the humanization of the gods, which goes hand in hand with an awesome esteem for the personal psyche in its concrete existence –

confrontations, reactions, immediacy. A psychology that is designated archetypal dare not be only a secular humanism and involvement is basic for all psychology, for all human existence, and hardly needs inflating by still more emphasis. The problems of the psyche were never solved in classical times nor by archaic peoples through personal relationships and "humanizing," but through the reverse: connecting them to impersonal dominants.

The dominants in the background permit and determine our personal case histories through their archetypal case histories, which are myths, the tales of the gods, their fantasies and dreams, their sufferings and pathologies. The plurality of archetypal forms reflects the pagan level of things and what might be called a polytheistic psychology. It provides for many varieties of consciousness, styles of existence, and ways of soul-making, thereby freeing individuation from stereotypes of an ego on the road to a self. By reflecting this plurality and freedom of styles within the structures of myth, the archetypal perspective to experience may be furthered. In this spirit *Spring* hopes to proceed.

Originally published in *Spring: An Annual of Archetypal Psychology and Jungian Thought* (1970).

1. R. Grinnell, "Reflections on the Archetype of Consciousness – Personality and Psychological Faith," *Spring: An Annual of Archetypal Psychology and Jungian Thought* (1970).

2. E.C. Whitmont, "On Aggression," *Spring: An Annual of Archetypal Psychology and Jungian Thought* (1970).

3. A. Guggenbühl-Craig, "Must Analysis Fail Through Its Destructive Elements," *Spring: An Annual of Archetypal Psychology and Jungian Thought* (1970).

4. T. Wolff, "Einführung in die Grundlagen der Komplexen Psychologie," in *Die kulturelle Bedeutung der komplexen Psychologie* (Berlin: Psychologischer Club Zurich, 1935), p. 7 (translation mine).

5. S. Freud, "Heredity and the Aetiology of the Neurosis," *Collected Papers* (New York: Basic Books, 1959), 1:148.

6. *CW* 7:410.

7. *CW* 16:115.

8. *CW* 8:325; *CW* 9.1:260.

9. R. Stein, "The Animus and Impersonal Sexuality," *Spring: An Annual of Archetypal Psychology and Jungian Thought* (1970).

Psychology:
Monotheistic or Polytheistic?

I

In the conclusion to his late work *Aion*, heavily preoccupied with Christian symbolism, Jung writes: "The anima/animus stage is correlated with polytheism, the self with monotheism."[1] Although he pays high respect to the "numina, anima and animus"[2] and conceives the self as a conjunction, he nevertheless also implies that as anima/animus is a pre-stage of self, so is polytheism a pre-stage of monotheism. Moreover, the self is "the archetype most important for modern man to understand."[3]

The preference for self and monotheism presented there strikes to the heart of a psychology that stresses the *plurality* of the archetypes. (Archetypal psychology begins with Jung's notion of the complexes whose archetypal cores are the bases for all psychic life whatsoever.) A primacy of the self implies rather that the understanding of the complexes at the differentiated level once formulated as a polytheistic pantheon and represented, at its best, in the psyche of Greek antiquity and of the Renaissance, is of less significance for modern man than is the self of monotheism. Were this all, archetypal psychology would be nothing but an anima fantasy or an animus philosophy. Explorations of consciousness in terms of the gods – Eros and Psyche, Saturn, Apollo, Dionysus – would then be only preliminary to something more important: the self. The self archetype would be paramount, and one should be investigating its phenomenology in the *quaternio*, the *conjunctio*, mandalas, synchronicity, and the *unus mundus*. The question "polytheism or monotheism" represents a basic ideational conflict in Jungian psychology today. Which fantasy governs our view of soul-making and the process of individuation – the many or the one?

The very sound of the question shows already to what extent we are ruled by a bias toward the one. Unity, integration, and individuation seem an advance over multiplicity and diversity. As the self seems a further integration than anima/animus, so seems monotheism superior to polytheism.

Placing the psychological part of this question to one side for the moment, let us first depose the ruling notion that in the history of religions or in the ethnology of peoples monotheism is a further, higher development out of polytheism. Radin devoted a monograph to this subject.[4] He concluded: "... as most ethnologists and unbiased students would now admit, the possibility of interpreting monotheism as part of a general intellectual and ethical progress must be abandoned..." (p. 24). He argues forcefully and cogently against the evolutionary view: that monotheism emerges from, or is later or higher than, polytheism or animism (pp. 29–30).

Radin bases monotheism not upon developmental stages, but rather upon the idea of temperament. Some people everywhere are by temperament monotheistic; they have a monotheistic psychology. "All the monotheists, it is my claim, have sprung from the ranks of the eminently religious" (p. 25). "Such people are admittedly few in number..." "It is the characteristic of such individuals, I contend, always to picture the world as a unified whole..." (ibid.). These are the theological thinkers, a small elite in any culture, sharing a common temperament, and their influence upon their brethren in the same culture is stubborn and effective.

The inexpugnable persistence of monotheistic religion could be psychologically accounted for by Jung's theory of the self. Then we might be tempted to conclude that monotheism is so strong because it is the theological equivalent of a more complete, integrated, and powerful (numinous) psychic condition. But already two objections crop up. First, Radin says monotheism "has obviously not been the triumph of the unifying principle over the disruptive" (p. 29). I take this to mean that religious and social order and disorder, unity and disunity cannot be correlated with monotheism and polytheism. Second, to base the strength of religious monotheism upon analogy with the psychologically more complete state of the self begs the same question, which is nowhere established: the superiority of monotheism to polytheism. Persistence does not necessarily demonstrate the superiority of monotheism, nor even its victory. Gray[5] points out that two varying attitudes toward God can exist at one and the same time; the monolatry of Yahweh did exist among the Jews (even as late as the Exile period) side by side with the worship of other deities.

Despite the historical evidence of religions, there is a fond notion without adequate foundation that monotheism is the pinnacle and that "the evolution of religion thus manifests, it would seem, a definite tendency toward an integration of our mental and emotional life..." (Radin, p. 6). Jung may not be borne out by the historical facts of religion, but he is borne out by the psychological bias of the historians of religion who put monotheism on top in the name of integration.

Two examples help to show this bias towards evolutionary monotheism. In his examination of the decline of Greek religion, Nilsson[6] finds the movement of religion from single, well-delineated gods to a multiplicity of powers and daimons a degeneration. The magic, superstition, and occultism that prevailed in later periods was, according to Nilsson (of Protestant Sweden), a disintegration. A century earlier, Schelling fantasied a vague *Urmonotheismus*, which developed later into a clearly formulated monotheism of the Old Testament as the highest product of religious consciousness. Between the first primitive monotheism and the later highly developed stage, there occurred Babel, which for Schelling represented the incursion of polytheism.

The hypothesis of the superiority of the self and monotheism over anima/animus and polytheism finds companions among historians of religion. Consequently, Jung's hypothesis may be one more expression of the theological temperament. This temperament has been more narrowly described as introversion, for Jung writes: "The monistic tendency is a characteristic of introversion, the pluralistic of extraversion."[7] As in other areas of human activity, Jung sees the two tendencies in theology, where they are expressed as monotheism and polytheism, to be also "in constant warfare."[8] Neither of these two attitudinal tendencies is superior to the other and neither is an evolution of the other. They are givens and given as equals.

So, too, we must keep distinct the ideas of individual and of cultural development, the self stage of the individual and the monotheistic stage of religion. It is nowhere established (despite E. Neumann) that the stages of religious thought (if there are such things, and Radin doubts it) necessarily parallel stages of individual consciousness (if there are such things). Moreover, according to Radin, we should not think in developmental terms at all about the kinds of religion. Culture and religion do not move upwards from the many to the one, from disorder to order, from Babel to Jahweh: monotheism is not identical with superiority except from within its own *Anschauung*.

The idea of superior monotheism, and progressive stages toward it, has been instrumental to the notion of a superior self, attained through the progressive stages of individuation. Now since monotheistic superiority is questionable, so the superiority of monotheistic models for the self should as well be questioned.

Perhaps linear thinking in stages is but another reflection of a monotheistic temperament whose Judeo-Christian fantasies favor historical development and hierarchical improvement, whereas the anima/animus and its model of polytheism tend toward a multiple field of circularity. Perhaps we should be less certain about stages of development in religion and in the individual and more questioning of the kind of consciousness that perceives in terms of stages.

Our argument has already turned psychological. We are no longer examining the religious evidence presented by Radin, but rather the psychological theory he proposes: that monotheism results from "an intellectual-religious expression of a very special type of temperament and emotion."

We have already suggested in these pages[9] last year which specific archetypal pattern tends to manifest in descriptions of the self. The self is personified as the Old Wise Man; its images are so often said to be ordering, e.g., geometric figures, crystals and stones, and abstractions beyond imagery; the behavior associated with the self and the process that leads to it is usually presented in the language of introversion, generic to "children of Saturn." From the viewpoint of an archetypal psychology "the special type of temperament and emotion" that produces monotheism and favors the self above anima/animus and views their relation in stages would be the senex. This archetype might also help account for theological monotheism's obdurate persistence, religious intolerance, and conviction of superiority. It might also account for the peculiarity of the self concept, which works symbolically to unite the realms of religion and of psychology into an indiscriminate whole. This leads to theological confusion about psychologizing God – a problem with which Jung was ever bothered. It leads also to psychological confusions about theologizing the psyche, producing dogmas, propitiatory rites, priesthoods, and worship. Likewise, the emphasis upon the self of psychological monotheism may help explain the theological interests of contemporary Jungians (as well as the Jungian interest of contemporary ministers) and the peculiar blending of analytical psychology with Christianity which we shall discuss below as the "Protestant direction."

II

What then about polytheism and the anima/animus? Let us first suspend monotheism, both in our theological judgments and our psychological convictions about stages, about unity and about linear and even spiral advancement. Let us also try to suspend the pervasive influence of our monotheistic desires for a utopia of integration (Kronos's Golden Age), and that fantasy of individuation that characterizes it mainly as a movement towards the Old Wise Man and that, by subtly obscuring the differences between psychological man and theological man, prepares the ground, in Radin's language, for a monotheistic elite of "eminently religious individuals…admittedly few in number." By putting in suspension the senex domination of our attitudes, we might regard polytheism afresh and *psychologically*.

Jung used a polycentric description for the objective psyche. He envisioned it as a multiplicity of partial consciousness, like stars or sparks or luminous fishes' eyes.[10] Psychological polytheism corresponds with this description and provides its conceptual formulation in the traditional language of our civilization, i.e., classical mythology. By providing a divine background of personages and powers for each complex, it would find place for each spark. It would aim less at gathering them into a unity and more at integrating each fragment according to its own principle, giving each god its due over that portion of consciousness, that symptom, complex, fantasy, which calls for an archetypal background. It would accept the multiplicity of voices, the Babel of the anima and animus, without insisting upon unifying them into one figure, and accept too the dissolution process into diversity as equal in value to the coagulation process into unity. The pagan gods and goddesses would be restored to their psychological domain.

We would consider Artemis, Persephone, Athene, Aphrodite, for instance, as a more adequate *psychological* background to the complexity of human nature than the unified image of Maria, and the diversity expressed by Apollo, Hermes, Dionysus, and Hercules, for instance, to correspond better with psychological actualities than any single idea of self, or single figure of Eros, or of Jesus or Yahweh.

Focus upon the many and the different (rather than upon the one and the same) also provides a variety of ways of looking at one psychic condition. There are many avenues for discovering the virtues in a psychic phenomena. Depression, say, may be led into meaning on the model of Christ and his suffering and resurrection; it may through Saturn gain the depth of melancholy and inspiration, or through Apollo serve to release the blackbird of prophetic insight. From the perspective of Demeter depression may yield awareness of the mother-daughter mystery, or, through Dionysus, we may find depression a refuge from the excessive demands of the ruling will.

This emphasis upon many dominants would then favor the differentiation of the anima/animus. Quite possibly – and now this is my claim and contention – closer interest in a variety of divine hypostases and their processes displayed in myth will prove more psychological, even if less religious (in the monotheistic sense of religion). This interest will more likely produce more insights into emotions, images, and relationships, even if it be less encouraging for a theology of evolutional wholeness. It will more likely reflect accurately the illusions and entanglements of the soul, even if it satisfies less the popular vision of individuation from chaos to order, from multiplicity to unity, and where the health of wholeness has come to mean the one dominating the many.

Polytheistic psychology obliges consciousness to circulate among a field of powers. Each god has his due as each complex deserves its respect in its own right. In this circularity there seem no preferred positions, no sure statements about positive and negative, and therefore no need to rule out some events as "pathological." When the idea of progress through hierarchical stages is suspended, there will be more tolerance for the non-growth, non-upward, and non-ordered components of the psyche. There is more room for variance when there is more place given to variety. We may then discover that many of the judgments, which have previously been called psychological, were rather theological. They were statements about dreams and fantasies and behavior, and people too, coming from a monotheistic ideal of wholeness (the self).

Monotheism or polytheism, self or anima/animus pose still another either/or: theology or psychology. Traditionally, psychology deals with the second order of things, i.e., the emanated world of flux, diversity, and the phenomenally imperfect. Its concern has traditionally been with the actualities of the soul, its modes of existence, its fantasies, emotions, and experiences, whereas theology considers the soul eschatologically, from the viewpoint of self. Wholeness defined by psychology means everything – all the phenomena as phenomena, things as the present themselves. Wholeness defined theologically means the one – things as they are in God. From this difference can arise two views of completion, a psychological wholeness where individuation shows itself as being what one is as one is, and a theological wholeness where individuation shows itself in degrees of approximation to an ideal of unity. The more I am occupied by the anima or animus the more I will be concerned with the welter of psychological phenomena. The more I am occupied by the self, the more will I show concern with goal states, peak experiences, and universality.

From this superior vantage point, Babel and the proliferation of cults in the Hellenistic period always seem a degeneration. Likewise an "animus court" and its ambivalence, or the multiplicity of dream women, become but an inferior pre-stage of unity. (Remember how the Prophets warn against the promiscuity and harlotry of Israel.) The many-faceted world of Olympus must fade before a single God (even if in three persons).

But one might also consider the proliferation of cults as a *therapeia* (worship, service, and care) of the complexes in their many forms. Then one could understand the psychic fragmentation supposedly typical of our times as the return of the repressed, bringing a return of psychological polytheism. Fragmentation would then indicate many possibilities for individuation and might even be the result of individuation: each individual struggling with his *daimones*. If there is only one model of individuation can there be true individuality? The complexes that will not be integrated force recognition of their autonomous power. Their archetypal cores will not serve the single goal of monotheistic wholeness. Babel may be a religious decline from one point of view, but it may also be a psychological improvement, since through the many tongues complete psychic reality is being reflected. So the current delight in superstitions, witchery, and oracles have a psychological significance even if they be considered inferior religion. Through these images and practices anima/animus aspects of the psyche begin to find traditional reflection and containment in an impersonal background. Without the gods, who offer differentiated models for the peculiar psychic phenomena of anima and animus, we see them as projections. Then we try to take them back with introverted measures. But "the individual ego is much too small, its brain much too feeble, to incorporate all the projections withdrawn from the world. Ego and brain burst asunder in the effort; the psychiatrist calls it schizophrenia."[11] Without a consciously polytheistic psychology are we not more susceptible to an unconscious fragmentation called schizophrenia?

Monotheistic psychology counters disintegration with archetypal images of order (mandalas). Unity compensates plurality. Polytheistic psychology would meet disintegration in its own language and archetypal likeness; there would be less need for compensation through opposites. The contrast between anima/animus and self appears in *Aion* as a contrast between pagan gods and the *imago Dei*. Of the anima/animus Jung writes:

> They are quite literally the father and mother of all the disastrous entanglements of fate and have long been recognized as such by the whole world. Together they form a divine pair, one of whom...is characterized by *pneuma* and *nous*, rather like Hermes with his ever-shifting hues, while the other...wears the features of Aphrodite, Helen (Selene), Persephone, and Hecate. Both of them are unconscious powers, "gods" in fact, as the ancient world quite rightly conceived them to be. To call them by this name is to give them that central position in the scale of values, which has always been theirs whether consciously acknowledged or not ...[12]

The self of psychological wholeness, briefly, more clearly reflects the God of monotheism and the senex archetype.

> Unity and totality stand at the highest point on the scale of objective values because their symbols can no longer be distinguished from the *imago Dei*. Hence all statements about the God-image apply also to the empirical symbols of totality. Experience shows that individual mandalas are symbols of *order*, and that they occur in patients principally during times of psychic disorientation or re-orientation. As magic circles they bind and subdue the lawless powers belonging to the world of darkness, and depict or create an order that transforms the chaos into a cosmos.[13]

Let me hasten to make clear that a polytheistic psychology is also religious. In following Jung we are regarding the anima and animus in their divine forms and are giving them "the central position in the scale of values which have always been theirs." Religion is not defined by the number of its gods, but rather in terms of the observance or binding of events to one or many gods. Relating psychic events to many gods and many powers and daimones should not be assumed to a lessening of the glory of a single high God nor on the other hand a broadening of the single high God into something bigger and better. We can get away altogether from "better and worse" once we leave theological thinking and its monotheistic bias, which sets the question in that kind of language. Polytheistic psychology has room for the preferential enactment of any particular myth in a style of life. One may be Protestant, or Herculean, or Dionysian, or a melancholic child of Saturn, according to the archetypal core governing one's dominant complex, and thus one's fate. And even the myths may change in a life and the soul serve in its time many gods. Polytheistic psychology would not suspend the commandment to have "no other gods before me," but would extend that commandment for each mode of consciousness. Then, each archetypal possibility of the psyche – including those we now call psychopathological – could follow its principle of individuation within its particular divine model. No one model would be "before" another, since in polytheism the possibilities of existence are not jealous to the point of excluding each other. All are necessary that they together serve one law only: necessity. Polytheism gives archetypal psychology a religious mode even for psychopathology by suggesting an adequate background in myth for each of the sufferings of the soul.

III

The theme monotheism/polytheism is immensely complex and packed with energy. The best minds of the early centuries of our era were obsessed with this issue and from that conflict of paganism with Christianity[14] our historical psyche and our psychological theory has been cast in what eventually became the current Protestant direction.

The essence of this direction reflects the Christian victory over the pagan world which can be summed up in a phrase from Gregory of Nazianzus who, while praising the pagans for their culture, epitomized the method for integrating it into Christianity: "...we take prisoner every thought for Christ."[15] The one God swallows all the others; Pan was dead because monotheism had conquered. The variegated natural totality (Pan) of the pagan world's modes of being together with their attributes and traits and kinds of consciousness were taken prisoner through binding them to the one central image and myth. Monotheism fed like Kronos on the gods it swallowed. As Christianity swelled, imprisoned "Greek philosophy [read psychology] sank exhausted into the arms of religion."[16] Even were we to grant that this historical event was beneficial for religion – and there are others besides Nietzsche who would grudge any value to this victory– it was not necessarily beneficial for psychology. This because specific patterns of consciousness mimetic to various Gods of the old pantheon were deprived of their archetypal backgrounds and imprisoned by the Christian model whose perspective now made them seem pathological. They could return but through the back door of mental aberration. A pathological view toward many of the psyche's phenomena is inevitable if psychology does not keep alive the totality of archetypal forms and their different ways of viewing the soul and life. Should psychology prefer instead to merge the many ways into a wholeness determined by monotheism, ego towards self, "single one to single One,"[17] will it not too – did it not already – sink exhausted into the arms of religion?

The Protestant direction of analytical psychology crops out in many large and small ways. Currently we see it in the emphasis upon love as a panacea, without differentiation of the faces of love and awareness of tradition in regard to its constellations; in the merit of hard work upon oneself; in the inculcation of a "strong ego" in therapy through the ennobling of choice, responsibility, commitment, and the consequent manipulation of guilt; in the trust in simplicity, naiveté, and group emotion; in an anti-intellectual, anti-logos bias where trust (*pistis*) in the "unconscious" or the "process" is enough; in an emphasis upon revelation (from dream, from oracle, imagination, psychosis, analyst, or from Jung); and in a peculiar combination of introverted religiosity and missionary popularization. We see it as well in the sole model for psychological suffering in which death's value is dislocated onto rebirth, linear process of gaining a better condition in exchange for a worse. This model fundamentally devalues the existential importance of depression and the descent into dissolution per se. Downward phenomena are good, not in themselves but rather because they offer hope for resurrection. It appears especially in the theological obsession with evil, which, let us recall, was not an issue in Greek polytheism. The Greeks had no Devil; each form of consciousness had its specific component of wrong-doing and tragedy. Evil was not a separate component but a strand so woven throughout everything that the "integration of the shadow" was already given in the patterns of life, rather than a task for an ego to do. And the Protestant direction appears in the notion of the "ego-self axis," the confrontation between them, the new midpoint as a new covenant, and "Christ as paradigm of the individuating ego."[18]

When our model of individuation is governed by monotheistic psychology in its Protestant direction, every fantasy becomes a prisoner for Christ. Every fantasy cannot help but find meaning in term of the one path, like the pilgrim on his progress towards integration. Even those that do not willingly fit in can be taken prisoner through the idea of a "pagan anima," a "chthonic animus," a "puer inflation," or the "problem of evil." These concepts bind psychic events to the dominant myth of the Protestant direction. Where once science, and then clinical pragmatics, were the enemies of the psyche, today the threat to the psyche's freedom of symbol-formation is nothing else than fading Christianity coming back in the guise of a theology of the Self to claim the soul for its own. Releasing the swallowed gods or the prisoners for Christ means realizing first how limited must be our hermeneutic for psychic phenomena when we have a monotheistic model for totality.

Jung has pointed out that "the extermination of polytheism" goes hand in hand with the suppression of individual fantasy, and as "the Christian idea begins to fade, a recrudescence of individual symbol-formation may be expected."[19] We may draw the conclusion that "individual symbol-formation" requires a polytheistic psychology, because the symbols refer to their likenesses in the variety of archetypal forms through which they find their authentication. Did Jung foresee that his stress upon totality and wholeness could be turned by the influential monotheism of our culture, and thus lead to a new onesidedness? The *imitatio Christi*, no longer a religious dogma or practice, becomes a psychological dogma subtly channeling the vital flow of individual fantasy back into the one old vessel, now called "wholeness."

Jung's contrast of the Christian with the polytheistic suggests a tension between them in his soul. In the tribute to Jung at his funeral, the minister spoke of Jung as a heretic. Jung's heresy, if we may follow his minister in calling it so, was however one of extension and revision, not of denial. He added a fourth to the trinity and therewith the dimension of psychic reality to Christian dogma. Therewith, too, the god within was re-affirmed. The experiential and phenomenological god of psychology included a fourth dimension, the underside of shadow, femininity, and the pagan past. He added to the Christ of orthodoxy the wealth of alchemical imagery, and like the Christian philosophers of earlier ages he connected his explorations again and again with the Christ image. Moreover, his description of the *imago Dei* as the Self follows the monotheistic model, by subsuming the many opposites under the highest goal, union. Sharper heresy was avoided.

The East[20] (where the self notion, the mandala and the Old Wise Man image are first at home) and alchemy provided ways around the desperate issue of heresy, which so obsessed the Renaissance giants and the more profound of the Romantics. Bruno, who posited a plurality of worlds, was forced out of the Dominican order and later burned; Ficino took another tack and in his mid-life was ordained into the Church's service.

Wordsworth's mystical pantheism declined into woolly support of established religion. Coleridge, immersed fully in the dilemmas of Neoplatonist polytheism (appearing in his day as pantheism), "regarded himself as an orthodox Church of England man."[21] The tension between his imaginal, sensuous life and his Christian convictions was said to have been at the core of Coleridge's private agony. Blake followed the method of Gregory Nazianzus by taking every fantasy into the Judea-Christian nexus. Those who started boldly into paganism – Shelley, Keats, Byron – died before the issue was fully upon them. Nikolai Berdyaev believed the issue insoluble.[22]

Is this also true in the realm of psychology? Is the restoration of the pagan figures to their place as archetypal dominants of the psyche impossible in a monotheistic psychological world? If so, then we must abandon our attempts at an archetypal approach based on polycentricity and accept analytical psychology a prisoner for monotheism in its current Protestant direction and let psychology sink exhausted where it may. The task of psychology, let us stress, is not the reconciliation of monotheism and polytheism. Whether the many are each aspects of the one, or emanations of the one or its hypostases and persons is discussion for theology, not psychology. So, too, attempts to integrate the anima/animus into the self (as, for instance, the notion of stages) tend also to be theological: they present theories in the senex mode for integrating differences into a single order. The result generally disfavors the plurality of individual differences.

The way out of this dilemma is perhaps less theoretical than empirical. Which pattern offers my psyche in the mess of its complexes better options for meaning? Heuristic pragmatic criteria have always been decisive in choosing between rival structures of consciousness. Constantine became Christian (and through him our civilization) because the new monotheistic religion then offered redemption to lost areas of his psyche, which the paganism of the time could not quicken:[23] "The pagan cults were nothing but a confused medley, very loosely bound together by the customary dedication to 'all gods.' They had no common organization and tended to break up into their atoms."[24] The independence of the Greek city states and of the Renaissance Italian cities, the cry of liberty in the name of paganism during the Romantic

Revolution, as well as the contemporary separatist movements show on the political level a psychological dissociation away from central authority. Translating these polytheistic and separatist phenomena into a psychological metaphor we have Jung's vision of the objective psyche where the atoms reflect the multiple sparks.

Monotheism evidently provided Constantine's psyche with the central focus then needed. Today, may not the situation be the reverse? Can the atomism of our psychic paganism, that is, the rash of individual symbol formation now breaking out as the Christian cult fades, be contained by a psychology of self-integration that echoes its expiring Christian model? If so, then indeed, the self is "the archetype which it is most important for modern man to understand." The answer hangs in the historical balance; and the scale, so loaded with recrudescent individual fantasies, is surely tipping away from monotheism's definition of order and its *imago Dei*. The danger is that a true revival of paganism as *religion* is then possible, with all its accouterments of popular soothsaying, quick priesthoods, astrological divination, extravagant practices, and the erosion of psychic differentiations through delusional enthusiasms. The self does not provide bulwark, since its monotheistic description and protestant interpretation leave too much out. But when the self can be re-imagined through a variety of ambiguous archetypal perspectives and less assuredly through the senex, consciousness can find containers for its individual symbol formations. To meet the revival of paganism as religion we need adequate psychological models that give full credit to the psyche's inherent polytheism, thereby providing *psychological vessels* for the sparks. They may burst into religious conflagrations when left psychologically unattended or when forced into monotheistic integrations that simply do not work.

The restoration of the gods and goddesses as psychic dominants reflects truly both the varied beauty and messy confusion, and tragic limitation, of the anima/animus, their fascinating multiplicity, their conflicts, their lack of ethical cohesion, their tendency to draw us deep through life and into death. Polytheistic psychology can give sacred differentiation to our psychic turmoil and can welcome its outlandish individuality in terms of classical patterns.

The elaboration of these patterns in psychological terms is yet to be done. We have still to understand Artemis and Persephone, Apollo and Poseidon, in terms of our soul-images and behavior. Although Jung did devote much space in his works to the divine couple and their configurations, and also to the personal aspects of the anima and animus in our lives, he concentrated mainly upon the phenomenology of the self archetype. The same thorough work needs to be done upon the anima/animus. But before this work can be done we would have to recognize their importance and see things from within their archetypal perspective, *i.e.*, in terms of a polytheistic psychology. Hence, the urging in these remarks. The idea of four stages[25] of the anima and animus, inspired mainly from Goethe and where progression moves away from the physical and toward the spiritual, is only an initial attempt at an anima/animus phenomenology in terms of classical mythology. Until we follow Jung in examining the differentiation of wholeness with the same care that he applied to the integration of wholeness, our psychology does not meet the psyche's need for archetypal understanding of its problems.

If there are other psychological options for our need I cannot find them. These ideas and their presentation leaves much unsatisfied, and so others who may see the question and its answers more clearly are invited to respond to this issue along lines laid out here.

Originally published in *Spring: An Annual of Archetypal Psychology and Jungian Thought* (1971).

1. *CW* 9.2: 427.
2. Ibid., 425.
3. Ibid., 422.
4. P. Radin, *Monotheism Among Primitive Peoples* (Basel: Ethnographical Museum, 1954; also issued as Special Publication No. 4 of the Bollingen Foundation).
5. C. Buchanan Gray, *Hebrew Monotheism* (Oxford Society of Historical Theology, Abstract of Proceedings for the Year 1922–23), cited by Radin, p. 22. On the polytheism that existed side by side with Greek monotheism, see M.P. Nilsson, *Greek Piety*, trans. H.J. Rose (New York: Norton, 1969), pp. 116–17 ("Monotheism"). Judeo-Christian monotheism in its conflict with Greek paganism, however, was tolerant of co-existence, cf. Nilsson, p. 124.

6. M.P. Nilsson, "The Dionysiac Mysteries of the Hellenistic and Roman Age," Volume 5 of *Skrifter utgivna av Svenska Institutet i Athen* (Lund: Gleerup, 1957). Cf. the last chapter of Nilsson's *Greek Piety.*

7. *CW* 6:318.

8. *CW* 5:149.

9. J. Hillman, "On Senex Consciousness," *Spring: An Annual of Archetypal Psychology and Jungian Thought* (1970). Reprinted in *UE* 3: *Senex & Puer,* pp. 242–61.

10. *CW* 8:388ff.

11. *CW* 11:145.

12. *CW* 9.2:41.

13. Ibid., 60.

14. *The Conflict between Paganism and Christianity in the Fourth Century,* ed. A. Momigliano (Oxford: Clarendon Press, 1963); see also E.R. Dodds, *Pagan and Christian in the Age of Anxiety* (Cambridge: At the University Press, 1965) for concise psychological characterization of the age and for references.

15. Gregory of Nazianzus, "In Praise of Basil" (*PG* 36, 508), quoted from J. Shiel, *Greek Thought and the Rise of Christianity* (New York: Barnes & Noble, 1968), p. 76. See further, B. Delfgaauw, "Gregor von Nazianz: Antikes und christliches Denken," *Eranos Yearbook* 36 (1967).

16. "Here knowledge is replaced by revelation in ecstasy. After Greek philosophy had performed this self-castration it sank exhausted into the arms of religion; as Proclus expresses in one of his hymns to the gods: 'And so let me anchor, weary one, in the haven of piety.'" E. Zeller, *Outlines of the History of Greek Philosophy,* trans. L.R. Palmer. (London: Kegan Paul, 1931), pp. 313–15, quoted from J. Shiel, *Greek Thought and the Rise of Christianity.*

17. "…this is the way to pray as single one to single one." Plotinus, *Enneads* V, 1, 6 (trans. Shiel), or "alone towards the alone" (trans. Mackenna). Cf. V, 9. 11: "solitary to solitary."

18. For basic formulations of the Protestant direction, see particularly the writings of E. Edinger: "Christ as Paradigm of the Individuating Ego," *Spring: An Annual of Archetypal Psychology and Jungian Thought* (1966); "The Ego-Self Paradox," *Journal of Analytical Psychology* 5:1 (1960); and "Ralph Waldo Emerson: Naturalist of the Soul," *Spring: An Annual of Archetypal Psychology and Jungian Thought* (1965), where we find (p. 97) the following passage: "In the process of assimilating the old culture to the new psychology, we discover again and again colleagues of the spirit. Emerson is such a colleague. He was a dedicated forerunner of the new world view that is only now beginning to reach its full emergence. The essence of this new view is well expressed by another colleague of the spirit, Teilhard de Chardin." The emphasis in both Emerson and Teilhard de Chardin is clearly upon a transcendental evolutionary wholeness. But Jung has been given many other

kinds of spiritual colleagues. In textbooks he is grouped with Freud and Adler; in his own writings we find suggestions that he looks back upon a spiritual line that includes Goethe, Carus, Kerner, and the French alienists of the nineteenth century; that abrasive scandal to authority, Paracelsus, and Nietzsche too, can be colleagues of the spirit. Jung has also been placed alongside of Tillich and Buber, called the true successor of William James, and given for spiritual colleagues the Masters of the East, Albert Schweitzer, the Gnostics, and others too numerous and irrelevant to mention. The fact that there are these many views regarding Jung and his work is further witness to his multiple psychology and the multiplicity of viewpoints, i.e., polytheistic psychology, in general. The Protestant direction is only one ray in the spectrum.

19. *CW* 8:92.

20. For one instance of the Eastern reinforcement of monotheistic psychology see Jung's "Psychological Commentary on 'The Tibetan Book of the Great Liberation,'" *CW* 11:798, beginning: "'There being really no duality, pluralism is untrue.' This is certainly one of the most fundamental truths of the East..."

21. T. McFarland, *Coleridge and the Pantheist Tradition* (Oxford: Clarendon Press, 1969), p. 220; see further, p. 223.

22. Cf. his *The Meaning of the Creative Act* (New York: Charles Scribner's Sons, 1936).

23. A. Alföldi, *The Conversion of Constantine and Pagan Rome*, trans. H. Mattingly (Oxford: Clarendon Press, 1948), p. 8.

24. Ibid., p. 12, where the presentation of the Christian victory over paganism is put altogether as a conquest by monotheism over polytheism.

25. On the four levels of the anima, see *CW* 16:361; on the four levels of the animus, taken from Faust, see E. Jung, *Animus and Anima* (Putnam, Conn.: Spring Publications, 2008), pp. 8–9. For an elaboration of the anima in terms of the Greek Kore figure, see *CW* 9.1:306–83.

Psychology:
Monotheistic or Polytheistic?
Twenty-Five Years Later

I

Twenty-five years ago, my essay "Psychology: Monotheistic or Polytheistic?" was a first attempt at revisioning depth psychology and its therapeutic practice, an attempt based upon very old, very tangled, and in some ways Florentine, roots of Western culture. That essay placed the dilemmas of psychotherapy in a cosmological context prior to Freud's nineteenth-century medical positivism and to Jung's Romantic origins and influences. Yet, it drew upon the same sources as they – the Greek and Roman mythic imagination, attempting to take these classical sources to their full implication, by exposing the inevitable conflict of that mythical imagination with the dominant one of Western culture: that of the Bible. I referred to this conflict in the manner of usual scholarship as one between Hellenism and Hebrewism.

This essay of twenty-five years ago sought to expand the psychology of the consulting room toward philosophy and mythology on the one hand, and on the other to turn the attention of therapeutic theory backward to the basic cleft in the ground of Western culture and which Western culture straddles, the clash between pagan and Christian, that is, between the Greek, Roman, Etruscan, Carthaginian, Celtic and Germanic imagination and the imagination of the Bible – Christian, Hebrew, Mohammadhan.

Further, I began there a review of the basic idea of diagnosis, the *Krankheitsbild* or "clinical picture" in terms of cultural illness, the sickness of images in our culture, owing to the long historical prejudice against images for their association with polytheistic paganism, or in monotheistic language: "idolatry and demonism." I urged the clinician to study not only the images of sickness but also this sickness of images.

As we all know this historical conflict persisted for centuries and was never laid to rest, resurrecting in poets and painters and composers who attempted to restore the ancient myths and gods, in folk festivals with their evident traces of Mediterranean paganism, and in the Church councils theological controversies over images, and the trials of heretics. All this is well known. That these same issues arrive in psychological practice, that this conflict between monotheism and polytheism is fundamental to depth psychology where the old pagan forces arise again, was less well known, although Freud and Jung opened our eyes to the myths in the pathos, the gods in the diseases. Both also wrote strongly against the unconsciousness resulting from Western religious thinking.

And, as you also know, in that essay of twenty-five years ago, I tried to rejuvenate the faded awareness of that war between monotheism and polytheism by throwing myself full tilt into the battle on the side of pagan polytheism. Though an old warrior, and living in a rural retreat, unlike Cincinnatus I have not retired from warfare.

What I did not then recognize and now begin to see is that a monotheistic vision informed my own eyes when reading and interpreting the monotheistic position. In other words, I was fighting in my martial manner – intemperate, unrelenting, and blind – not as an old Roman Pagan but with the very, almost fanatical, attitudes of what I was attacking! I was acting as a monotheist even while defending polytheism. I took the Bible – Hebrewism, Christianism – with the very literalism that I accused it of.

How would a pagan read those pages? To answer, I do not want to turn back to the Origen/Celsus arguments – largely anyway obliterated by Christian censorship – or the discussions in the Renaissance by Pico and others who tried to amalgamate and resolve in subtle ways all these differences.

Rather I want to demonstrate how we can review, revision even, fundamental Biblical tales in such a way that our method of reading and the meaning emerging from the reading happily accords with a pagan feeling. By this "pagan feeling" I mean a style that welcomes myth, personification, fantasy, complexity, and especially humor, rather than singleness of meaning that leads to dogma. Now, when we turn to the

Bible it will be with an eye freshened from twenty-five years of mythical sensibility and metaphorical understanding.

II

To show you what I mean by this re-reading, let us look at four particular passages, all of them rather crucial for the Western religious traditions. For example, the Fifth Commandment (Exodus 20:12): "Honor thy Father and thy Mother." Why in the world does this appear tucked in the middle between the four great theological ordinations that come first and the societal prohibitions of the last five commandments about murder, adultery, theft, perjury, and envy?

I believe this fifth commandment is precisely placed and holds the first part and last part together. If we read the text (Deuteronomy 5:16), this commandment establishes the personal parents as guarantors of fate. It reads: "That thy days may be prolonged and that it may go well with thee, upon the land which the Lord thy God hath given thee." The parental injunction continues the elimination of "other gods," the local, pagan, immanent gods of the land, and replaces them with your personal parents.

Parents have been elevated to the position of ancestor spirits: they bestow long life and protect from early death; like invisible daimones, they bear good fortune ["that it may go well with thee"]; finally, like pagan nature spirits they are attached to the land, the earth belonging not to them but claimed as his, by the transcendent God above.

Once the relation with the local ancestral spirits is replaced by human parents, then a moral code for a social contract must be spelled out – the final five commandments. In a pagan world, the moral code is upheld by invisible forces, articulated in rituals. Societal order depends on the ancestors, gods and daimones and lesser animated powers who take part in human affairs and keep them in a lawful order.

In place of ritual and taboo, we are given commandments; in place of ancestor spirits, personal parents.

A narrow reading, a literal reading, sees only the reduction of the pagan protectors and bestowers of life to ordinary human parents. As well, this narrow reading sees the human parents exalted to supra-human dimensions. This cosmic position of the Father and Mother reinforced by the place of the commandment following directly upon the first theological four defining God and his worship, affects our theories of therapy to this very day. Parents are honored in every therapeutic system as the determinants of each case history. The fifth commandment thus becomes the basis of humanism and secularism and the narrowing of the idea of family to hereditary relations.

But there could be a wider, more generous reading – a pagan reading. It would say that we can find a father and a mother in all things that prolong your days, wherever things go well with thee, and parenting may be discovered in the place, the land, the earth where we inhabit. Such would be a more environmental and animistic way of honoring the Father and the Mother, and would deliver your actual parents from having to carry in their persons the exaggerated burdens of your destiny – the length of your life and its fortune.

The Second Commandment, my next example, is even more subtle to read. It seems so clearly a prohibition of the pagan mode of worship, the pagan mode of thinking in images. The text reads: "Thou shalt not make unto thee a graven image, nor any manner of likeness, of anything that is in heaven above, or that is in the earth beneath, or that is in the water..." (Exodus 20:12).

Very clear and straight forward – no imitation of nature, no likenesses. Don't focus on nature if you are going to pay attention to God. God is very jealous of images of nature, maybe of nature itself – for in the next line, God says exactly this. Don't pay obedience to nature because I am "a jealous God."

But then this most curious event occurs. Moses comes down from the mountain "with the two tables in his hand; tables that were written on both their sides ... and the tables were the work of God, and the writing was the writing of God, graven upon the tables ... (Exodus 32:15). You can see an icon of these tablets in most any synagogue anywhere. The very commandment that says "no graven images" is graven on an image by God himself and becomes a graven image.

Even more subtle, more perplexing: God does not ban images as such – fantasy images, dream images, the images such as Ezekiel saw. It is the graven kind, the fixed, chiseled, or what I am calling literal.

God seems to warn less against images than against literalism, saying, in brief, "Don't take your images literally."

What kind of trick is God playing here?

How else read these seemingly straight directions except as strange conundrums? They present subtle twists that displace the subject and deconstruct the first literal meaning. Such twists we nowadays call "jokes" and which may be the *fons et origo* of Jewish humor.

For instance, two stories of Abraham (Genesis 17, 18, and 22). Abraham is the great traditional patriarch, God's most devout servant, pious, righteous, a true believer. God has to put him to the test, of course, because God doesn't seem to believe anyone – not Abraham, not Job. Anyway, God demands a demonstration of faith from Abraham. Take your little boy Isaac up the mountain and slay him for a burnt offering, showing your devotion beyond all human attachments.

Clearly what God asks doesn't make sense. The future generations would come from this son, God's whole chosen people. It's not only short-sighted, it's horrible. An atrocity. But good old Abraham goes right along with the plan; gets up early in the morning, cuts some fire wood, and goes where God told him to go. He laid the fire and bound his son upon it, and had his knife at the ready. Just as he was about to kill the boy, he was stopped by the voice of God. Lo and behold, right behind them a ram was caught in a thicket, which then became the sacrificial offering.

Abraham, in his literal understanding of God's will had to be stopped by God himself, who was, in effect, saying: Hold it, old man! Don't take me so literally. This murder of your boy is not what I meant. I want you to dedicate your son, to offer your son, recognize your son's sacrality, but not *kill* your son! You have to hear through my messages, that's why I sent the angel, to intercept you. You have to hear the *angel* in the words; the invisible *angelos*, the message, not just the literal words.

What Abraham had to give over and kill off was the thick-skulled, ram-headed quickness in his mindset that gets caught up in the thickets of literal understanding.

The second story of Abraham shows him again needing a lesson about literalism. This story seems more to do with Sarah his wife and her conception of Isaac. They were both very, very old; and, as the text says: "It had ceased to be with Sarah after the manner of women." When God informed her that this couple "well stricken in age" would bear a child, Sarah laughed – "After I am waxed old, shall I have pleasure, my lord being old also?"

When Abraham hears this pronouncement from God that Sarah will give birth to their child, Abraham laughed too and "said in his heart: 'Shall a child be born unto him that is a hundred years old?'"

Their laughter gives earnest commentators much to worry about – especially Sarah's laugh. Is it a laugh of mockery and irony and plain disbelief – like saying, "Get on with you God, don't be pulling my leg. Don't make fun of an old women who has no son." Mockery as "laughing at" is how the word laugh is generally used and especially in the Gospels (Matthew 9:24; Mark 5:40; Luke 8:53), referring to scornful disbelief in the words and acts and prophecies of Jesus.

Or is the laughter in Sarah already a sign of fertility? An indication of crone wisdom in her – like that of Baubo in Greece and the Oni witches in Japan? Her sexual fantasy is very much alive – speaking to God about *edna* (pleasure), as if it would be impossible with such an old husband. Although her natural time had passed, she had knowledge of the unnatural aspect of sexual fantasies and their procreative power. And Abraham too had to work through the naturalistic fallacy, the literal limits on his imagination of creativity.

The marvelous detail in this story is less the fertility marvel as such than the fact that both of them – 90 and 99 as the Bible states – laughed, and produced a child. Clearly, the laughter and the fertility belong in the same image, and, note well, *laughter comes first, preceding procreation.* Laughing produced the child, and that's why its name, Isaac, derives from the Hebrew root, "to laugh." And – I draw your attention to this further exegetical particular: laughter and fertility are joined *only* in this image. No one in the whole big good book has such good laughs.

Monotheism cautions us *not* to laugh, and the words translated as laugh and laughter in both Greek and Hebrew generally mean "laugh at," deride, mock; only Eccleiastes says there is a time for laughter and that one of these times is feasting and celebration – such as we are doing today. Otherwise, Luke warns: "Woe unto you who laugh now, for ye shall mourn [6:25]; and James [4:9] writes: "Be afflicted, and mourn, and weep; let your laughter be turned to mourning...."

That's about it! There is praise and jubilation, but no good laughs. No smiles either – a word for "smile" doesn't even appear! (Remember the tradition that the Greek gods smile, especially Aphrodite, called "the smiling one").

But Abraham and Sarah – they laugh. For them, God is telling a dirty joke, like the sort we still hear about old people and their ribald fantasies.

By the way, a little excursion for Biblical scholars who may be uncomfortable with my exegetical style. The word *edna*, translated "pleasure" in the Jewish Bible and the King James Bible, is *voluptati* in the Vulgate of Jerome. It is, however, altogether excluded, the phrase not appearing at all, in the Septuagint. Today probably, *edna, pleasure voluptati* would be translated by French Freudian Feminists as *jouissance*, that is, if they look into that patriarchal text at all.

III

Now, with the mighty authority of the Bible to back us we may turn to the attack on literalism, my favorite enemy. I have called literalism the enemy in various writings. It is still the danger, the disease endemic to psychology. The god in this disease is monotheism – even if not the god whom the monotheists refer to, since that god, as we just saw, plays tricks and makes jokes, and tries to teach his beloved patriarch, Abraham, about multileveled understanding.

The disease of literalism comes with writing, that is, when images are graven. This is the deep prophetic implication in the second commandment: Moses, you are going to get all this written down, and therefore henceforth your followers are going to be the people of the book. Moreover, that sect coming along later known as Christians are going to write sacred books of their own, one of which announces "In the Beginning was the Word, and the Word was with God, and the Word was God." That is, giving to the word the utmost divine omnipotent authority. Of course, the Bible says God doesn't begin with "the word." He begins with *making distinctions* about light and dark, above and below, etc., and also with *mythical tales* about mythical places, like Eden, and mythical animals and people like Adam and Eve.

Myths have no "authorized version" as the main Protestant Bible is called in the English-reading world. Myths are best authorized on the authority of their teller. Oedipus is told by Sophocles, but also by Voltaire, Cocteau and Freud; Ulysses's wanderings by Homer, but also by extraordinary authors such as Joyce and Kazantsakis. Myth allow many versions; myth contains many versions; myth requires many versions. No *graven* images.

However, when a pagan like D.H. Lawrence tells a Jesus story embroidered with unauthorized details, or the filmmaker Martin Scorsese presents his invention of the "Last Temptation of Christ" — these versions are heresy.

An authorized version, sanctified as Holy Writ, is essential to all monotheistic literalism. Simply said: God himself speaks in the book; the book is God's word, is God in verbal form. Yet the God we have uncovered in the two Abraham tales breaks the naturalistic fallacy of fertility, and even deconstructs his own clear instructions to Abraham by producing the ram in the thicket in place of Isaac. It would seem God is not the literalist that orthodox monotheism would wish him to be. Or, perhaps he deconstructs his own message as if he likes to joke.

IV

Lest we become too literal ourselves — always the risk in a martial discourse — let us return to smiles and laughter. For it is the laugh, a primal laugh not a primal scream, that brings together our main themes: Hebrew monotheism, Hellenic paganism, and psychoanalysis.

First, we may remember that one origin of depth psychology is Freud's great Jewish joke book, one of the thickest and longest of all his treatises. Freud, however, owing to his Hebraic tradition got something backwards. He read the jokes for their instructive lesson, their secret hidden meaning. A pagan influenced psychology reads secret hidden meanings as a joke. Not what is hidden in a joke is sexual innuendo; but hidden in sexuality is grand comedy, and which provides the stuff through the ages for comedies such as the bedroom farce. As the poet W.H. Auden wrote in his "New Year Letter" (1940):

> ...truth, like love and sleep, resents
> Approaches that are too intense,
> ...through the Janus of a joke
> The candid psychopompos spoke.[1]

Sarah understood this, but Freud didn't. Yet, today, how we laugh at the subterfuges of Freud regarding Martha and Minna, and at the ridiculous material of those early cases and their comic figures: Little Hans, the Wolfman, Dora, Anna O., Irma's Injection. All taken so intensely by those scientifically deliberating bearded men of Vienna and the non-drinking clinicians and serious women devotees in Zurich.

The reduction of the pompous to the humorous, the conversion of the sexually hidden to a joke (rather than the joke to the sexually hidden), is what Charles Boer and I tried to exhibit with our own little joke, *Freud's Own Cookbook*, so brilliantly turned into Italian by that hidden master, Vittorio Serra Boccara, and published by Cortina some ten years ago. That book, a seemingly simple parody of Freudianism and the serious history of psychoanalysis, is actually an exemplary text of the pagan view. It claims the laugh is essential to meaning, the deepest meaning brings a smile, a laugh and is therefore closer to the nature of the Id and to redemption of personality from the oppression of a laughless biblical superego than any other mode of "becoming conscious." The Bible itself considers the laugh redemptive, as in Psalm 126, when Zion is restored then the "mouth is filled with laughter" or as Luke says (6:21): "Ye shall laugh later," that is, in the afterlife, in heaven.

To the propositions that laughter is redemptive, that it cures the insanity of literalism and that the God of monotheism himself jokes I summon evidence from an incarcerated madman, John Perceval. I reported on Perceval in my *La vana fuga dagli Dei*.[2] Perceval, an Anglo-Irish practicing Christian, and the son of a British Prime Minister, went into a religious paranoia in the 1830s and was locked away for three years, during which he suffered all sorts of delusions, including hearing God's instructions and commandments – like Abraham and Moses. He wrote in detail about them in his diaries (London 1838–40), edited by the eminent philosopher Gregory Bateson and published as *Perceval's Narrative* in 1961.[3] Here is what Perceval says:

> I suspect that many of the delusions, which…insane persons labour under consist in their mistaking a figurative or a poetic form of speech for a literal one…the spirit speaks poetically, but the man understands it literally…the lunatic takes the literal sense (pp. 270–71)…it does not follow that things seen in the spirit are to be practised in the flesh (p. 307).

As if Perceval were addressing Abraham, he writes:

> Lunacy is also the mistaking of a command that is spiritual for that which is literal – a command which is mental for one that is physical…the intention was…not practically to put the words in execution (p. 279).

As his cure progressed, he "obeyed the spirit of humour" because "the Deity…often intimates his will by jesting…" We may let revelations, epiphanies, prophecies descend without believing, or disbelieving, them. *Serio ludere* said the Renaissance maxim.

Reflecting upon his three years in the madhouse, Perceval presents at the end of his narrative his theory of lunacy.

> I conceive therefore that lunacy is also a state of confusion of understanding, by which the mind mistakes the commands of a spirit of humor, or of irony, or of drollery;…that, perhaps, this is the state of every human mind…I mean that in the operations of the human intellect, the Diety…often intimates his will by thus jesting…that in the misapprehending or perverting of this form of address may consist original sin (p. 281).

The original sin, then, is not the fall from grace owing to what the Church Fathers called "the animal mode of generation" and what Freud called the libidinal Id, that is universally basic to human nature. Rather the Fall is the fall from metaphor, the fall into literalism. The Paradise lost is the loss of the sense of humor so that you are no longer able to get God's jokes. As Perceval's cure progressed, he said he "obeyed the spirit of humour," whereas while he was deluded he was obeying the will and word of God. *Fiat mihi.* I believe Perceval not only was cured, but converted. I think he came our of the asylum with a pagan mind.

V

All along I have been using the word "pagan" quite freely. I like the word for my own self-referent reasons – and it offers us another joke: One meaning of *pagos* in Sophocles and Euripedes is "rocky hill"; *paganos*, people of the rocky, hilly countryside. A pagan is therefore a *hill-man*.

The Latin *paganus* was used originally in several ways: to refer to native peoples who were civilians and peasants and not members of an alien army. "Pagan" was used in distinction to others, particularly to the *alieni*, that is, members of foreign militia who came into native villages and towns throughout the Roman world, armies composed of Mithraic and mainly Christian soldiers. Thus as one writer explains:

> *Pagani* or pagans are quite simply "people of the place." Town or country, who preserved their customs, whereas the *alieni*, the "people from elsewhere," were increasingly Christian...[This] defines paganism as a religion of the homeland in its narrowest sense: the city and its outlying countryside. And it predicts the diversity of pagan practices and beliefs.[4]

This basic meaning – "people of the place" – opens one more radical distinction between the two cosmoi we are contrasting. The pagan mind will not submit easily to abstract universals, the logic's of science, of mathematics, to general laws. It would find alien the idea of a one, true, and universal religion as the Roman Church has defined itself.

It would be alienated by the placelessness of virtual reality and cyberspace, an internet of websites that is not actually sited, anywhere local and physical, and whose images are not attached to or framed by an environment. The pagan, as I understand its psychology, abjures universals altogether including nationalism and ecumenicalism, unless they be qualified by the particular place where the universals are effective. That's why the ancient gods and goddesses were always place specific, with epithets that located them and brought out their specific local qualities. The Artemis or Hermes or Apollo of one place was not the same Artemis and Hermes and Apollo of another. Hence, "a diversity of pagan practices and beliefs."

Therefore it is so difficult to translate lectures such as this because translation not only raises the question of languages, but that of transferring a mind and a soul from one place to another. All translations are traitorous and treacherous, because they assume what is said in one place can be said anywhere. The Christian missionaries taking the one true word to tribes around the world found they had to compromise the universality of their creed to accord with "the people of the place."

The logic of monotheism attempts to override place. This logic favors a cosmos of space and time, the cosmos of Descartes and Newton and Kant, a single and empty abstraction that can contain all things. The difference among things are merely differences of motions and coordinates. Places, like everything else – tastes, smells, colors that qualify the world – are only "subjective, " not inherent in things, but given to them by humans. Accoding to Immanuel Kant, the most influential of all modern universalists, the good taste of the wine does not belong to the wine but to the subject that enjoys it.[5] Tell that to a Tuscan contadini, Immanuel!

This devastation of the world as a sensory living body and the reduction of place to vast and unqualified space has led us to the architectural and ecological catastrophes we now suffer. A world that is sheer *res extensa*, of course, obliterates pagans, "the people of the place," and so we find peoples fighting for place with insane passion as in Ireland, Kurdistan, Palestine, Yugoslavia, and in the Sudan and Timor where war between polytheism and monotheism has killed hundreds of thousands.

The definition of pagan as people of place, as defenders of place against the alienation brought by monotheism, explains to me – twenty-five years later – how and why my work has turned so actively to environmental, ecological, and urban concerns. It is the logical outcome of my pagan disposition. Environmentalism is simply paganism in today's world. The active defense of particular sites, the localism, the championing of rivers and forests, the protection of animals and tribes against intruders from universal corporations and abstractions of government – all this is paganism in contemporary dress. The Greens and the Environmentalists will die for a dolphin or a tree. This is religion, even if without the old gods.

It would be more conventional to regard my ecological concerns of the last five years as a return to the world after the descent into the nether regions, and the burning of the bridge to the day-world with which I opened my book *The Dream and the Underworld*. This would be a Jungian reading of my ecological turn. After the *nekyia*, the introversion; the psyche moves out to the "other." But this explains a human life in terms of a developmental formula in accordance with the path of individuation. Is this not a monotheistic reading? A reading that puts us all on the same one path – first half of life, second half; inward follows outward and vice versa; compensation.

Rather, my polytheism belongs to my character as a "hillman," a pagan. My earliest excitement in philosophy came from reading Plato at the university in Dublin and Plotinus at the university of Zurich, and from the overwhelming emotional impact that the physical places of Greece and Sicily had on me, unlike any I have felt anywhere including the Himalayas or Jerusalem. It was never hard for me to sympathize with Freud in regard to his pathological incident on the Acropolis, and with Jung's fainting at the Zurich railroad station intending to go to Rome to which he never came. Particular places have singular spirits, and they call us.

The particular spirit that calls us in this place is that of Machiavelli. He speaks directly to the martial tone with which I opened this discourse, promulgating between monotheism and polytheism. Machiavelli, sardonic or sincere, we cannot know for sure, said (*Il principe* XIV):

> Debbe adunque uno principe non avere altro obietto né altro pensiero, né prendere cosa alcuna per sua arte, fuora della guerra...
>
> (A prince should have no other thought or object, nor should he occupy himself with anything else, than war...)

The war that has lasted through the ages need not be understood literally, nor Machiavelli, either. I read him and understand war in the sense of Heraclitus, who said "war is the father of all things." It generates heat, focuses attention, stimulates passion, activates ideals.

By thus charging the atmosphere, Mars draws forth Mars's companion Venus, who softens the edges, that sweeter yielding that allows us to see in the Christian Percival a pagan understanding of God and to find, in the Sufi songs and verses and cosmologies and in Kabbalist expositions and midrashes of Jewish monotheism, a polysemous, multilayered diversity of images, metaphors, daimones, and personifications that are quite pagan.

We should remember in regard to this Mohammadan and Jewish diversity that place plays a definite role. Diversity of understanding derives from diversity of place – the Rabbi's are identified by the mullahs with Cairo or Safed or Minsk or Gerona or Cordoba or Baghdad, some local school that gives the reading of the Torah and Koran a distinct flavor, much as the therapy school of Vienna differs from the school of Zurich, though both are reading the same text: the psyche.

Despite my caveat against taking war too literally and my appeal to Venus, we must never cease playing this "mono-poly" game, for the mind is always in danger of succumbing to philosophies of oneness and to the tyranny of unification in every sort of sphere. Therefore the pagan perspective must always be kept in mind, and with it the devotion to places, their spirits and daimones, the singularity of colors and smell, the taste of the wine and the sound of the speech of each distinct locality. For it does not matter to which church we go, to which god we kneel, or none at all, or how we imagine the next world, so long as we do not neglect the sensate diversity of this world and the local gods who inhabit it, who bless it with flavor and color, a delight to the eyes in spring and the nose's joy, this incredible richness of each local springtime, restoring us for a short season to Eden – and *eden* by the way, is directly related to *edna*, that Hebrew word for Sarah's "pleasure."

Originally published in *Spring: A Journal of Archetype and Culture* 60 (1996).

1. W.H. Auden, *The Collected Poems*, ed. E. Mendelson (New York: Vintage Books, 1991), p. 206.

2. J. Hillman, *La vana fuga dagli Dei*, trans. A. Bottini (Milan: Adelphi, 1991).

3. *Perceval's Narrative: A Patient's Account of his Psychosis, 1830–1832*, ed. G. Bateson (Stanford: Stanford University Press, 1961).

4. P. Chuvin, *A Chronicle of the Last Pagans*, trans. B.A. Archer (Cambridge: Harvard University Press, 1990), p. 9.

5. "Der Wohlgeschmack eines Weines gehört nicht zu den objektiven Bestimmungen des Weines ... sondern zu der besonderen Beschaffenheit des Sinnes an dem Subjekte, was ihn genießt." I. Kant, *Kritik der reinen Venunft*, A29.